Mastering Cognitive Behavioral Therapy

Strategies for Overcoming Anxiety, Depression, Borderline Personality Disorder, PTSD and Trauma

(A Complete Guide to Psychotherapy)

Copyright 2018 by Michael Garron - All rights reserved.

This book is geared towards providing precise and reliable information, with regard to the topic of cryptocurrency and its related topics. This publication is sold with the idea that the publisher is not required to render any accounting, officially or otherwise, or any other qualified services. If further advice is necessary, contacting a legal and/or financial professional is recommended.

From a Declaration of Principles that was accepted and approved equally by a Committee of the American Bar Association and a Committee of Publishers' Associations.

In no way is it legal to reproduce, duplicate, or transmit any part of this document, either by electronic means, or in printed format. Recording this publication is strictly prohibited, and any storage of this document is not allowed unless with written permission from the publisher. All rights reserved.

The information provided herein is stated to be truthful and consistent, in that any liability, in terms of inattention or otherwise, by any usage or abuse of any policies, processes, or directions contained within, is the solitary and utter responsibility of the recipient reader. Under no circumstances will any legal responsibility or blame be held against the publisher for any reparation, damages, or monetary loss due to the information herein, either directly or indirectly.

Respective authors own all copyrights not held by the publisher. Abraham K. White is referred to as the author for all legal purposes, but he may not have necessarily edited and/or written every single part of this book.

The information herein is offered for informational purposes solely, and is universally presented as such. The information herein is also presented without contract or any type of guarantee assurance.

The trademarks presented are done so without any consent, and this publication of the trademarks is without permission or backing by the trademark owners. All trademarks and brands within this book are thus for clarifying purposes only and are the owned by the owners themselves, and not affiliated otherwise with this document.

978-1-9992202-7-3 (Paperback)

Published by Pluto King Publishing

Table of Contents

Introduction 20
    Basic Points to Consider 22
    Basic Considerations to Note 22
    Who Can Benefit From CBT? 23

Disclaimer 25

Chapter 1 – What Is CBT and Cognitive Psychology? 26
    The Principles of CBT 27
    What General Efforts May Work? 28
    The Basic Concept of Cognitive Psychology 30
    Background 31
    Information Processing Is Key 32
    Questions to Ask 34
    Cognitive Psychology vs. Behaviorism 35
        Reflexes 37

Chapter 2 – The Value of CBT and Cognitive Psychology 38
    Identify Thought Processes 38
    An In-Depth Study 38
    All Aspects of Behaviors are Identified 39
    Retraining 39

More Organization over Life 39

No Medication Needed 40

What About Issues? 41

Chapter 3 – The General Steps and Stages of CBT 43

Assessment 43

Therapeutic Alliance 44

Explore the Thoughts 44

Awareness Is Vital 45

Review Negative Things 46

Reshaping Thoughts 47

An Example 47

Chapter 4 – The Value of Memory 50

Working Memory 51

How Long Does Working Memory Last? 52

Decay or Interference? 53

Long-Term Memory 55

Procedural Memory 56

Semantic Memory 56

Episodic Memory 57

Is Long-Term Memory More Important Than Working Memory? 59

- Neurons and Their Impact on Memory 59
  - Unfamiliarity Is Vital 60
  - Are Negative Issues Stronger? 60
  - Childhood 61
- What Are the Oldest Memories? 61
- Chapter 5 – Metacognition 63
  - About Metacognition 63
    - The Three Main Types of Knowledge 64
    - Déjà Vu 65
    - Cryptomnesia 66
    - Imagination Inflation 68
    - Validity Effect 69
    - False Fame Effect 70
  - How Well Are Concepts Managed in Metacognition? 71
  - Introspection Is Key 72
    - An Emphasis on Realism 73
  - How Are Sparks of Interest Formed? 73
- Chapter 6 – The Importance of Perception 75
  - Interpretation 76
  - Structuralism 76
  - Why Perception? 77

Chapter 7 – Using CBT to Handle One's Perception 79

  Identifying Self-Image Issues 79

  Seek Outside Help 80

  Adjust Perception Based on Feedback 82

  Consider the Habits of Other People 83

Chapter 8 – How Attention Works 85

  How This Relates to Perception 85

  Top-Down vs. Bottom-Up 86

  Visual or Auditory? 87

  Change Blindness 88

  Inattentive Blindness 89

  Selective Attention 90

    How Selective Attention Impacts Fears and Moods 91

  Divided Attention and Multi-Tasking 92

Chapter 9 – Identifying How Someone Pays Attention 95

  The Dot-Probe Test 95

  The Emotional Stroop Test 96

  The Visual Search Test 97

  Why It's Important to Test Attention 97

Chapter 10 – Resolving Issues Relating to Attention Through CBT 98

  Take the Long Road 100

7

- Can This Work for Those With ADHD? 100
- Chapter 11 – The Most Common Cognitive Distortions 101
  - The Basics of a Distortion 101
  - Filtering 101
  - Black and White Thinking 102
  - Magnification or Minimization 103
  - Overgeneralization 104
  - Jumping to Conclusions 104
  - Personalization 105
  - A Desire to Be Right 105
  - The Fallacy of Change 106
  - Heaven's Reward Fallacy 107
  - Resolving Distortions 108
- Chapter 12 – Fact vs. Opinion – How to Manage Both 110
  - What Causes a Person to Misconstrue Facts and Opinions? 110
  - The Basic Test 111
  - The Main Goal 112
- Chapter 13 – The Learning Experience 113
  - How Are Ideas Introduced? 113
  - Actions Become Automatic 114
  - How Long Can Memories Last? 115

A Note About Learning 115

Chapter 14 – Triggers and Causes 117

    Triggers 117

        Can Added Time to Think Make Triggers More Severe? 118

        How Can a Trigger Be Identified? 119

        Can Multiple Triggers Occur At the Same Time? 119

        How to Decide Which Triggers Are the Most Intense 120

    Causes 121

    The Value of Healing 122

Chapter 15 – Understanding Fear 123

    A Basic Consideration of Fear 123

    What Causes Fears to Develop 124

    Association With Certain Things 125

    The Amygdala 126

        The Hippocampus 126

        The Prefrontal Cortex 127

    Fears Developed in Youth 127

        Adult Fears 129

    Signs That Someone Is Afraid 130

        Can Being Quiet Suggest Fear? 132

    Understanding Fears 132

The Feararchy 133

How Fears Can Impact Perception 135

When Are Fears Produced? 136

Chapter 16 – Trauma and How It Can Be Reframed 138

The Definition of a Trauma 138

Effects of a Trauma 140

The Value of Resiliency 140

Can Trauma Truly Be Erased? 141

Reframing the Trauma 142

How Does the Trauma Help? 142

Chapter 17 – Repressed Memories - How to Access Them 145

Why a Memory Becomes Repressed 146

The Concern of Imagination Inflation 147

How to Identify a Repressed Memory 147

How Can These Memories Be Recovered? 148

An Authenticity Warning 151

Chapter 18 – How Cognitive Behavioral Therapy Controls Fears . 152

Realistic Thinking 152

Create Challenges to Negative Thoughts 153

Preparing Self-Statements 154

Additional Questions to Ask 155

Chapter 19 – Using the Fear Ladder For Managing Intense Fears 157

   A Progressive Approach 157

   How to Produce the Fear Ladder 153

   An Example of the Fear Ladder 159

   How Many Steps? 161

   How Much Time? 161

Chapter 20 – Exposure Therapy to Control Smaller Fears 162

   Exposure Therapy Differs From the Fear Ladder 162

   How to Enter Into Exposure Therapy 163

   How to Tell If the Fear Is Too Intense 164

   Calming Exercises for Exposure Therapy 165

   How Often to Exercise? 167

Chapter 21 – Exposure and Response Prevention – A Solution For OCD-Related Fears 168

   A Focus on OCD Fears 168

   Get to Know a Fear 169

   Planning a Chart 170

   Working With the Fear Ladder 171

   Managing a Fear With OCD 171

Chapter 22 – Replacing Stimuli 174

   An Example 175

How Long Does It Take to Respond To the New Stimuli?.......... 176

Chapter 23 – Socratic Questioning to Curtail Irrational Thinking 177

    The Overall Goal 182

    A Secondary Socratic Approach for Private Concerns................. 182

        How to Do It 183

        Should Other People Be Consulted Anyway? 184

    Chapter 24 – Understanding Anxiety.. 186

    What Makes Fear and Anxiety Different?..................................... 186

    Commonplace Worries About Anxious People............................. 187

    Common Anxiety Disorders.. 188

        Separation Anxiety 189

        Social Anxiety Disorder 189

        Generalized Anxiety Disorder 190

        Panic Disorder... 190

        Worries About Help or Escape.. 190

        Selective Mutism... 191

        Post-Traumatic Stress Disorder 192

    Can a Single Plan Treat Any Kind of Anxiety?............................. 193

Chapter 25 – Causes of Anxiety.. 194

    Social Situations... 194

    Job or School Problems 194

Financial Worries 194

Traumatic Events 195

Physical Conditions 195

Chapter 26 – Control Anxiety by Tolerating Uncertainty 196

Signs of Intolerance 196

Avoidance Coping 197

Resolving Intolerance 197

Chapter 27 – Identifying Ruminations 201

What Makes a Rumination Likely To Develop? 201

Goal Progress Theory 201

Response Style Theory 202

Types of Ruminations 202

Thoughts When Ruminating 203

A Process to Identify Ruminations 203

Chapter 28 – Cognitive Defusion to Control Anxiety 205

When Does Cognitive Defusion Work? 205

How to Use Cognitive Defusion 206

Preparation 207

Chapter 29 – Recognizing Intrusive Memories 209

Characteristics of Intrusive Memories 209

Addressing Memories 211

Chapter 30 – How To Become Mindful to Ease Anxiety 213

    Exercise Ideas for Mindfulness 216

    How Long Does Mindfulness Take? 217

    The Physical Effects of Mindfulness 217

    Can Mindfulness Occur Right After a Triggering Situation? 217

Chapter 31 – Progressive Muscle Relaxation 219

    The Steps 219

    How is the Body Targeted? 221

Chapter 32 – The Art of Positive Criticism 222

    How Positive and Constructive Criticism Differ 223

    Using Positive Criticism 223

Chapter 33 – Addressing Anxiety Head-On Through Rational Emotive Behavior Therapy 225

    Background of REBT 225

    Managing the Routine 226

Chapter 34 – Understanding Depression 229

    What Causes Depression? 229

        Genetics 230

        Impacts In the Brain 230

        Hormonal Changes 230

        Seasonal Affective Disorder 230

    Stresses in Life 231

    Moments of Grief... 231

  The Depression Cycle... 232

  Common Effects to Watch For 233

  What Are the Long-Term Effects? 234

  Men or Women? 235

  Can Depression Be Cured?.. 235

Chapter 35 – Dialectal Behavior Therapy................................. 236

  Reversing the Depression Cycle 236

  The Many Parts of DBT 236

Chapter 36 – Scheduling Pleasant Events 239

  Why Does This Work for CBT?... 239

  What Types of Events Can Work?....................................... 239

  Discovering New Skills 240

  Managing Activities.. 241

  What About Responsibilities?.. 242

Chapter 37 – Successive Approximation to Manage Depression .. 244

  The Basic Approach.. 244

  Good to Handle Fears 245

  Prepare Sub-goals... 245

  Review the Triggers.. 246

- Decide Where to Start 247
- Progressively Move Forward Through the Goals 247
- After Everything Is Finished 248
- How Much Time? 248

Chapter 38 – Anger and How CBT Corrects the Situation 249
- Recognizing the Body's Response to Anger 249
- What Causes Anger? 250
- Acknowledging the Anger 251
- Review the Anger 251
  - Short vs. Long-Term Help 252
- Be Removed From the Situation 252
- Consider the Alternatives 253
- Practice Happiness or Positive Thinking 254

Chapter 39 – Managing Grief Through CBT 255
- The Basics and the Classic Five Stages 255
- The Three Main Types of Grief 256
  - Common Effects That Accompany Grief 257
- Using CBT to Handle Grief 258
- Preparing a Goodbye Worksheet 260
- Be Willing to Forgive 261
- Be Willing to Forgive the Self 261

Invite New Things into One's Life 262

Emphasize Positive Memories 263

An Essential Note 264

Chapter 40 – The Art of Journaling 265

Creating a Journal 265

An Example of Journaling 268

What Types of Topics Can Be Covered In a Journal? 270

Chapter 41 – Forming Alternative Actions 271

Chapter 42 – The Validity Test 273

How Many Variables? 275

How Much Time Is Needed? 275

What If the Idea Is Invalid? 275

Chapter 43 – The Art of Visualization 277

How to Use Visualization 277

Chapter 44 – An Exercise in Positive Thinking 231

Three Simple Steps 231

An Example 282

What If a Negative Thought Occurs? 282

When Does This Work? 283

Chapter 45 – Reframing Disappointment 284

Make It Normal 284

17

The Main Goal 286

Chapter 45 – Final Tips for CBT 287

    Always Have a Goal 287

    Every Situation Is Unique... 287

    Determine the Proper Definitions 287

    Never Blame Others 288

    Never Be Overly Judgmental 288

Chapter 46 – Should a Psychiatrist Be Consulted? 290

    The Effort Is Overwhelming 290

    Obsessions Become Too Prominent 290

    Repeated Thoughts of Consulting a Therapist 291

    People Talk About One's Need For a Psychiatrist 291

    Feelings Aren't Getting Better.. 291

    Concerns about Medication 292

Conclusion 293

Introduction

It is through emotions that people can communicate with each other and make decisions about what they can do in their daily lives. Without emotions, life does not have much meaning. It is through emotions and understanding how they develop that a person's life can change or be influenced in some way.

It is difficult to predict the emotions that people may have on an average day. It only takes a few moments for one emotion to switch to another. No matter what emotions one experiences, they will add up throughout the day to create experiences that are truly unique for every person. Everyone has their own fears, worries, and concerns that influence what they do in their lives. The unpredictability that comes with life can be inconvenient for anyone, but it is also a problem that produces fears in many people. It is often a challenge to control those fears and keep them from being unmanageable. A person's fear might be crippling so that it becomes impossible to engage with other people or have a healthy attitude.

Anxiety can also be crippling; a person might start worrying about the things that may or may not happen. There are often times when that anxiety is unwarranted. The concerns people have can evolve into more significant concerns. People might become depressed over what is happening in their lives. They might feel as though they have no control over what they can do. Even worse, it is next to impossible for a person who is depressed to find a way to resolve the issue and to feel better without help.

Others might become angry and hostile toward others. They might become hostile toward people to where it would be impossible to work with them. The difficulty can be dramatic at times as an angry person can become violent. Those who have been struck with grief often do not know what they can do to resolve the sorrow that they feel. These emotions are issues that anyone could develop. They are problems that keep people from feeling better about who they are or what they have to do. More importantly, they are issues that might be unrealistic. These include problems where people are fearful and afraid or upset for no real reason at all.

There is a solution that may work for those who want to understand their emotions and resolve issues that hinder having a productive and happy life. This solution is cognitive behavior therapy, a popular study that is a vital evolution in the field of cognitive psychology.

Cognitive psychology is a study that focuses on how the human brain works. It concentrates on what inspires people to act in certain ways and behave. Instead of looking at the events surrounding what may cause a person to act in certain ways, cognitive psychology looks into what causes the mind to act as it does. This is about how people associate certain concepts with different values or ideas that they might hold.

Through the use of cognitive behavioral therapy, people can find ways to keep their mental faculties in check. This includes understanding what can be done to resolve problems and issues in one's life.

This guide explains how cognitive behavioral therapy can be utilized to control fears, depression, anger, and other common problems that may persist in one's life. With cognitive psychology, people can do more with their lives and know what they can do to manage their attitudes.

Basic Points to Consider

The world of cognitive psychology and behavior focuses on many aspects of life. It relates to a person's attention, memory, perception, and how people think about their own emotions. Through cognitive practices, it becomes easy for people to understand what can be done to manage different situations in their lives.

This guide delves into many important points relating to cognitive behavior therapy including:

- How the brain manages memory and attention and how it relates to cognitive functions

- Identifying what causes certain emotions to develop

- Steps for managing some of the problems people have in their lives

Knowing how to manage the human mind through CBT is a necessity. The practice includes a review of how the mental processes one holds may be supported and controlled.

Basic Considerations to Note

The practices listed in this guide include several that focus on the positive things that can come from cognitive behavioral therapy. These include several points that support the needs that people have for handling their lives:

- To learn how to replace negative thoughts with positive ones.

- Some physical exercises, particularly ones involving calming the body and mind to produce a sense of relaxation.

- Ways to plan one's life and to manage and encourage positive feelings.

- Several strategies for identifying feelings and how to replace or adjust them. Such strategies may help people recognize problems and identify what is causing certain feelings and emotions to develop.

All of these points are accompanied by detailed procedures and some examples. The information in this guide is meant to help people organize their attitudes and to grow stronger.

Who Can Benefit From CBT?

Cognitive behavioral therapy is a popular practice that focuses on how the human mind behaves and what causes a person to change and behave in certain ways. The points covered in this guide are valuable for all applications in one's life. This book may work for cases, such as:

1. Family Life

People often become worried about what will happen to their children or what might occur if certain events take place within a family unit. Cognitive therapy helps people handle those worries. The psychological analysis involved should help to understand many issues that may come along with managing life in general.

2. Romance

Romantic relationships are often filled with many concerns relating to the partnership between two people. Sometimes a person might become angry or grief-stricken if a romantic link is broken. By using many principles listed in this guide, it will become easier for people to avoid the fears they have and to move on when something does not go as expected. In fact, psychology helps to identify what causes a person to feel a certain way about the attitudes that one has toward falling in love.

3. School

School is important for all people regardless of how old they are. The anxieties that people have over tests, presentations, group events, and other things can be crippling. It is through cognitive psychology that these problems are managed.

4. Professional Life

Regardless of the workplace, it can take just a moment for people to become fearful and concerned about the situations they encounter. People often struggle with presentations or might be afraid of big meetings or events. Some might be depressed or angry when they don't get the jobs or opportunities they want. Those mental hang-ups can be controlled.

5. Public Life

It is understandable why people are often fearful of public settings. Everyone will have to manage these public situations at some point or another. This guide covers details on how people can handle their public lives and keep themselves from failing or struggling. Getting beyond the fear, anxiety, or any other concern one has is vital for ensuring life can be its best and not become more of a struggle than what it has to be.

Disclaimer

Although the points listed in this guide are used to manage fears, depression, and other mental issues, everyone will respond to these procedures and concepts differently. Some people might be able to control themselves sooner, while others might require extra help. The results that happen by following this guide should not be interpreted as being universal in nature. Any person subjected to cognitive behavioral therapy and other concepts relating to cognitive psychology must be monitored accordingly.

There may be some cases where a person may need to contact a psychiatrist for additional help. This could include cases where someone might not respond as well to CBT or if the person's emotions or mental state is intense or extreme.

Chapter 1 – What Is CBT and Cognitive Psychology?

People are often worried about psychological processes, and it is understandable. People think that psychological practices might not always work for them. The truth is that it is necessary to discover how such efforts can be of help to understand emotions and the possible causes. The most important part of managing psychological efforts is they are designed to be informative and helpful. It is through the intense monitoring of one's mind that it becomes easier for a person to succeed in life.

Part of psychology today entails the use of the study of managing fears. This can be helpful through the use of identifying what causes fears but also understanding how the brain responds to fears and how it might have produced them in the first place. Understanding these points works through what is known as cognitive behavioral therapy. It is a practice that helps a person to feel more confident and to understand the connections within the brain.

The ability to use cognitive behavioral therapy to resolve fears, anxiety and other common problems can make life easier. It is critical for people to understand what CBT is and how it can make a difference in one's life. CBT focuses on looking at how the brain functions and what causes a person to behave in certain ways. This includes a review of what causes a person to become afraid of things, hostile toward others, or otherwise difficult. The practice of cognitive psychology and cognitive behavior therapy is one of the cornerstones of mental health. This is a study about the mental functions and involves recognizing how the brain puts many concepts and thoughts together. The dense and detailed layout of the study makes it one of the most indispensable parts of psychology.

The Principles of CBT

To see how well CBT works, it helps to understand the primary principles of the practice. These principles relate to how well a person is capable of functioning in society. The overall goal is to change how a person thinks. By working with such practices, it becomes easier to think positively and to have a more controlled mindset.

The principles of CBT include the following:

1. Many mental problems develop from one's thoughts. These include improper thoughts or methods that are unhelpful and could be harmful to a person's sanity and safety.

Sometimes these thoughts are the result of not being familiar with certain ideas or concepts or from incorrect responses to the threats and worries that people encounter in their daily lives. The role of cognitive behavioral therapy is to help people understand why they think in certain ways. Every behavior is inspired by some stimuli or event that took place.

2. People develop negative mental issues due to how they have learned unhelpful or unsupportive behaviors.

People learn most behaviors in childhood. Those who struggle emotionally and cannot handle certain mental functions are more likely to exhibit unhelpful behaviors that only add chaos to their lives. Part of this is due to misconceptions or other false beliefs. They have clouded their minds with false information.

3. The main goal of managing mental issues is to learn how to cope with them.

CBT is not designed to be a straightforward cure. Many emotions that people have are next to impossible to relieve altogether. However, over time, CBT may help to alleviate some of the worries people have about their fears, feelings, and attitudes. This can help to reduce the intensity of anxiety, depression, fears, and other problems people have. CBT helps a person to acknowledge the emotions and feelings one has over time and to replace those feelings with new ideas or beliefs. Having the power to get those old thoughts out of the way is vital.

4. Negative problems and thoughts have to be gradually replaced over time. CBT helps a person to find new ideas to replace the old problems.

CBT helps alter the thoughts and impressions a person has and to have positive thoughts rather than negative. Knowing how to control those problems and to have a better mindset, in general, is the key principle of CBT.

What General Efforts May Work?

CBT efforts include many that focus on how the human body and mind can be supported:

1. A vital part of CBT is the ability to reevaluate the problems that one is in.

It is easy for the human mind to start thinking about certain problems based on what is true versus what is untrue. People have to reevaluate their ideas by comparing their values with what can be found in reality. Those who avoid the problems they encounter are only going to hurt themselves as they do not directly understand what they are dealing with. The fear and worry that is produced will only become worse and often harder for a person to solve and get over unless the right emotional and mental changes are made in the process.

2. Motivations have to be discovered.

People often make the wrong assumptions about some of the events and situation they come across in their lives. Sometimes the motivations are identified by what can be observed and may not be a true assumption. Knowing the truth about a stimulus or function is a necessity for one's success in managing emotions. Those who follow the truth will feel happy with themselves and confident in their abilities to manage their emotions accordingly.

3. A person's ability has to be utilized.

A reason why so many people become fearful or depressed is that they do not recognize the abilities they have. They do not understand that they can control most of what happens in their lives. Part of this involves knowing what can be done to control one's mindset and to ease one's thoughts before they can become unwieldy or hard to manage.

4. Calming and relaxing the body is critical.

Sometimes it is important to discover how the human body can be relaxed and tensions eased. It is often a challenge to relax and feel at ease for two reasons. First, efforts to relax might not be focused. Second, a person might feel that resting is not an active approach to resolving the fears and worries. Being calm involves more than just managing the physical body. It is also about knowing how to feel comfortable with the attitudes and feelings one has.

5. Finding new ways to think is vital.

The old ways of thinking might cause a person to have significant mental worries. Being capable of controlling how a person thinks is essential for managing one's worries or threats.

6. Replacing the old thoughts one had is even more important.

As great as CBT is to help people develop new thinking patterns, it is even more important to discover how to make those patterns work in lieu of the old ideas. There comes a need to replace the old thoughts with new ones that are more suitable. The new thoughts have to be compared with the old ones. Sometimes this requires a person to recognize that the new thoughts might be more relevant to one's life than what was used before. Having a better sense of control over how those thoughts are produced helps keep the attitudes and thoughts one has in check and is essential to understand what is happening in the human mind.

The Basic Concept of Cognitive Psychology

CBT is linked to cognitive psychology. This practice is one of the more essential studies to review regarding how the human mind functions.

Cognitive psychology focuses on how the human mind processes information. The goal of the study is to review how the mind responds based on memories, the attention produced, beliefs, and other vital points.

There are several points of cognitive psychology:

1. A person's memory has to be explored. This includes understanding how memories are produced and what makes them stronger or weaker. How memories may be repressed can also be explored.

2. The language that a person uses may be analyzed based on the mental capacities of that person.

3. A person's ability to pay attention can also be factored into the process. This includes looking at how someone's attention can be managed.

4. Problem-solving is also important to review - how people resolve issues based on their emotions and other stimuli that they encounter.

Background

Cognitive psychology has been a tried and true part of studying the human mind for generations. In fact, the study of how the brain manages thoughts has been around for thousands of years. Cognitive psychology gets its roots from much of the history of psychology. Plato proposed in the 4th Century BC that the brain was what prompted mental processes. It was not until the middle part of the 20th Century that cognitive psychology would be recognized as a study to take seriously.

Behaviorism had been used as a study for years. The concept of behaviorism suggested that it is through one's environment determines what one's emotions are or how that person will act in certain situations. Although many in the scientific community felt that behaviorism to be valuable, there existed a desire to see what causes the mind to associate certain concepts with particular feelings or desires.

The number of procedures the human brain goes through to process feelings or emotions is diverse. Sometimes the feelings generated are directly due to certain stimuli. In other cases, a series of steps are used to produce certain feelings. Cognitive psychology identifies everything that causes a person to think in a certain way when encountering particular stimuli.

It was not until the 1960s when the term was first coined. Ulric Neisser created the term and focused in on many points:

- Cognitive psychology is based on how the human senses are processed.

- It focuses on how memories and beliefs are produced based on a person's history.

- It also concentrates on how particular feelings and emotions may be triggered based on the connections and values someone has developed in one's life.

The development of cognitive psychology remains one of the most essential developments in the field of psychology. It is through cognitive psychology that people understand how others might act and behave while understanding the intense processes that the human brain goes through. How the human brain works is more complex than what many know. It is through cognitive psychology that a person can explore the inner workings of the human brain. This all leads into CBT and how it may be used.

Information Processing Is Key

A person has to understand how different people process information in various ways. The brain's ability to process and use information helps to understand how thoughts and actions are produced. In the early 20th Century, Edward

Tolman proposed learning is not based on reading or studying but rather through the relationships that a person has between certain stimuli. A cognitive map may be formed within a person's brain to determine what one is learning and what that person's relationship to the subject matter might be.

The mind will take in data and will process it while creating relationships between this data and other items. Sometimes the relationships are based on emotions or how certain concepts may be influenced by others. As the age of computing evolved, it became clear that the human brain can be compared to a computer. A series of steps may be used in the information processing:

1. Things may be observed in one's local area. These include anything that might cause a person to feel certain emotions or have certain attitudes.

2. Various faculties within the brain will manage and process the content one encounters.

These faculties are one's short-term memory, one's ability to pay attention, and how one perceives things. All people respond to these concepts differently.

3. The brain will adjust or transform the content being explored into one of several unique methods.

People may start to link certain items with negative experiences, thus causing them to develop fears or to become anxious about what they encounter. Others might concentrate more on the positive aspects of what they encounter, thus associating those items with good feelings.

4. As stimuli are presented, certain emotions or attitudes are triggered.

The human brain is like a computer in that it takes in new data and finds a way to save and secure it. Through this processing, it becomes easier for a person to handle certain ideas and concepts in one's brain. The brain's ability to process information is at the forefront of CBT. Whether it is linking ideas or finding new ideas to replace old ones, CBT is a necessity for handling the functions and attitudes one has.

Questions to Ask

Cognitive behavioral therapy asks multiple questions about how people behave. Getting the answers to these questions is vital to understand how people might behave and what can be expected:

1. How does a person use reason?
2. Why does someone make certain decisions?

The decisions that a person makes are often based on situations, feelings, past events, and much more.

3. Why do people make errors?

Most people do not make errors on purpose. They have their own mental faults and worries that cause them to keep doing things in a certain fashion. CBT helps to understand the errors that someone makes and what might cause those issues to occur.

4. What causes people to remember certain things?

Sometimes this comes from positive memories or maybe from something disturbing that makes a person want to avoid certain stimuli.

5. Why do people fail to remember things?

It is through the decay of thought that someone forgets something that was proposed or introduced a while ago.

6. Why would a person misremember?

Different things happen when recalling memories or even storing them. Memories are especially critical for cognitive psychology as they relate to the influences in one's life.

7. How are certain meanings attached to various concepts or events in life?

Many feelings based on past experiences or attitudes that someone has. CBT considers those experiences and what can happen in general.

8. What motivates people?

9. How much time does it take for someone to transition from one emotion to the next?

This question concentrates on the learning process to manage emotions and it can be used to analyze what causes people to act in certain ways. The roots of what causes people to think certain things and to feel specific emotions can be unraveled, which can lead to better treatments.

Cognitive Psychology vs. Behaviorism

CBT and cognitive psychology are often seen as improvements over the art of behaviorism. Cognitive psychology concentrates on how people process and arrange information. This includes associating certain stimuli with particular feelings or memories. This branch of psychology focuses less on visible behavior and more on the decisions people make and the memories they produce. Behaviorism is the opposite in that it focuses not on how the mind organizes data but rather on the behaviors that are directly observed. People associate specific events with consequences that link to them.

For instance, let's say Susan is not interested in riding a bicycle. People may observe her trying to ride one but she keeps crashing as she cannot keep the bicycle balanced. Susan might notice many scenes of people crashing their bicycles and even worry about the sounds that might happen. In the case of cognitive psychology, one might assume that Susan is afraid of riding a bicycle because of the fear that she will continue to crash and hurt herself. She may associate a bicycle with harm and think she could be seriously injured while riding. Susan's case is different if you consider behaviorism. In this case, Susan could be given the option to use a bicycle or a car to get to where she wants to go. She may choose to use the car. While the car might be too much for a short distance, she would opt for the car instead of the bicycle because she knows it would be dangerous for her to get on the bicycle.

Behaviorism states that Susan acquired her feelings toward bicycles from the interactions she had with them. She directly contacting a bicycle and did not have a good experience with it. Cognitive psychology goes on a different route and suggests that she thinks a bicycle would not work out well. It is through her prior experiences and feelings that she struggles to handle a bicycle. Cognitive psychology delves into not only the things that someone sees but also the things that have been planted in one's mind. The key is to look at how the stimuli can influence one's thoughts and attitudes in some fashion. Even more importantly, it focuses on the objective feelings that someone has about a certain concept.

In short, behaviorists only look at observable behaviors. CBT practitioners look into every aspect of the human mind. CBT may be used to analyze how behaviors change over time. The same could be said about behaviorism, but that study would focus more on the change in the stimuli, not the mind. CBT focuses on the changes in one's mind and how a person's thought processes change.

Reflexes

Although cognitive psychology is a major evolution over behaviorism, there is one aspect of behaviorism that is still important to note. With cognitive psychology, reflexes are not considered. This refers to the sudden thoughts that a person might have and the attitudes one may hold over something observed. Reinforcements are not going to account for every behavior. Therefore, it might be difficult to understand what is happening within one's behavior over what is being reviewed.

Every event has stimuli and processes that change how people operate. Reflexes will change the behaviors that someone expresses, thus requiring a sense of control over how a situation may work out. Those reflexes may also evolve as time goes on. Some of the thoughts will be different after a while due to the changes that one encounters.

Chapter 2 – The Value of CBT and Cognitive Psychology

CBT and cognitive psychology are valuable aspects of mental health as they focus on many special points. It is essential to see how the human mind can benefit from cognitive psychology.

Identify Thought Processes

CBT is about understanding how people think and act. People are often capable of managing different emotions based on the attitudes they hold and the prior events that they have been subjected to. The behaviors people exhibit are due to their experience of certain situations and stimuli. It is through CBT and cognitive psychology that a person's mental faculties and capabilities are analyzed based on the thoughts people have. Part of this involves how people pay attention and how people learn new ideas. The general focus that one has and the more significant or traumatic experiences one has had in the past can play a part as well. No matter what the issues might be, it is essential for people to notice how well CBT can work based on how thought processes are managed.

An In-Depth Study

Behaviorism is useful as it allows people to identify what causes people to behave based on certain surroundings. While it does answer a few questions about what someone might do, it is not as detailed a study as CBT. CBT goes further into the human brain to determine what causes people to think in certain ways. The senses are focused while prior beliefs and memories may play a role. The physical surroundings of a person are only a small part of the study. In short, think of CBT and cognitive psychology as a natural evolution of behaviorism and how it identifies what someone might be thinking.

All Aspects of Behaviors are Identified

On the surface, a person's behavior might be analyzed based on a few basic concepts. A person's behavior can be analyzed based on what someone sees or does. There might be a legitimate reason for why someone does something that can be noticed. There is also a chance that behaviors might occur thanks to how the human brain processes ideas. CBT is used to review not only the behavior itself but also the source. The goal is to review all the thoughts that create behaviors to determine certain problems that someone might have. Having control over behaviors assists in identifying what is causing a person to think and feel a certain emotion.

Retraining

Retraining is a critical aspect of CBT to control what someone is thinking and how certain ideas may develop. Knowing how to retrain one's mind and keep it under control is critical for managing one's life and having a better attitude toward controlling certain issues and problems. The retraining process might take an extensive amount of time to complete. The practice is still worthwhile because it gives people extra control over how they manage their thoughts and how they concentrate less on the negative aspects of their lives and more on the good things that make life worthwhile.

More Organization over Life

People who have hard times often struggle due to how their lives are not as well organized as they might wish they were. People often struggle because they are too busy thinking about some of the problems they are having. Their thoughts are not well organized. CBT assists people in managing more things in their lives and deciding what they want to do. Using CBT, a person will have extra control over their functions in life. Part of this includes knowing how to manage emotional concerns and worries that one might develop. The ability to organize one's thoughts and to keep them under control without losing one's attitude or sense of stability is vital to one's success in any situation.

No Medication Needed

One thing that many people do to help them get over depression, fear, and other negative mental emotions is to use medications. Various medications are provided to people to control their brain functions. This could help people avoid the effort to change their lives. Medications to manage emotional issues can become a significant threat to one's mind and health. The fact that such medications often cost more money than what people can afford to spend only makes them worse and harder to bear.

CBT works well to assist a person to manage one's attitudes through natural processes and by creating new analytical points to consider. As appealing as medications might be to some people, they are only going to mask the issues that someone is experiencing. Knowing how to control one's mind through therapy is better as it creates long-term results.

Sometimes medication might result in a dependency that makes it harder for a person to function. The dependency occurs as the brain becomes used to the medication and cannot function without it. The medication will make life harder to manage in some of the worst cases due to the added stress on the brain. As frustrating as this can be, it is a problem of medication that often hurts people. Therapy assists the brain in finding ways to be in control to prevent such medications from being a threat to someone's life.

What About Issues?

Some of the issues that may occur in the cognitive psychology process are:

- People who struggle with learning disorders or difficulties might have a harder time benefiting from this process than others.

CBT entails a need to concentrate and to see how well the mind evolves. Those who cannot handle the concepts introduced might struggle to stay positive and happy about what they are doing with their lives.

- This only works with the problems that an individual has.

As useful as CBT can be for managing one's own mental issues, it is not necessarily something that will work for one's entire family. This is a strictly centralized concept that requires a person to stick with certain values and thoughts.

- It is unclear as to how long it would take for CBT to work. It might take years for CBT to be effective and useful to a person.

It is through CBT that it becomes easier for a person to have a controlled and functional life. Those who participate in CBT sessions will learn more about what they can do to grow and to be better, stronger, and happier people. More importantly, this keeps issues relating to fear, anxiety, and other problems from being a dramatic concern.

- Sometimes certain conditions might be too significant and a person may need more extensive help.

A person who is suffering from extreme depression and might experience suicidal thoughts or actions would have to receive advanced forms of treatment and support including treatments, hospitalization or advanced monitoring.

How Much Time Is Needed?

Everyone responds to cognitive therapy differently. Some people might do better with psychological reviews as they become comfortable with their doctors or more adept at some of the procedures used. The CBT process can take weeks or even months to complete. Extensive retraining within the brain is needed to make the most out of a practice. It is up to the participant to decide what one wants to get out of the process and how extensive the retaining work might be.

Those who are patient and willing to work at it will benefit the most from what CBT has to offer. It is through one's work and plans for CBT that it becomes easier for that someone to grow and thrive as a better individual. Of course, there are problems that come with CBT, but the positives surrounding the practice are much greater than any negative issues. It is exciting for people to notice how well CBT can work and how effective it might be in any situation.

Chapter 3 – The General Steps and Stages of CBT

Those who wish to utilize CBT should think about what they are doing when entering into the field. This is a practice that is very complicated and entails lots of effort on a patient's end. But those who are capable of thriving and evolving will grow into being better people. The steps in CBT can be extensive and in some cases complicated. It is through CBT that a person can evolve and be a stronger individual.

Assessment

The assessment is needed to identify a troubling situation at the start of the CBT process. Every person has his or her own situation that might be causing mental issues. The situation can be anything that someone might be struggling with. For instance, a person might be concentrated on things like being afraid of a certain idea or situation. That person could also express unreasonable anger toward others or certain situations.

CBT creates a strong alliance between the participant and anyone who might help. Whether it is working with a therapist or simply talking it over with other people or even with the self, it becomes easier for CBT to be effective when a friendly and fair assessment is used. The assessment process can take as long as necessary. The goal is to have a clear idea of what someone is thinking and how those thoughts or actions might change in order to recognize what someone might be doing with life and how it can all be organized.

Therapeutic Alliance

A therapeutic alliance is produced in the assessment process. It is where the person who undergoes CBT will feel confident about the process and will trust anyone who wants to help. This sense of trust is vital as it relates to how positive one's attitude might be and how strong the process will work. The trust may come in the form of anonymity or from a sense of compassion. The key is that a person will feel comfortable talking with someone to the CBT process. Knowing how well the process will work and receiving a simple introduction into it is vital to have a better experience with managing one's emotional issues and concerns.

There may be times when a professional administers the CBT process and might ask for outside help. This is for cases when a person has significant issues and poses a risk of self-harm or harming other people and needs additional help with managing the emotional or mental issues.

Explore the Thoughts

The next stage is recognizing and evaluating the thoughts one has. The assessment should have determined what the problems are. It is now time to go in depth to see what has caused those problems to evolve. The goal in this situation is to determine how the troubling situation started. CBT focuses on the concept in cognitive psychology where a person might start to feel discomfort or worried about things in life due to past events. Sometimes it could occur due to a physical injury, a divorce, a death in the family, a terrible experience in school or the workplace, or anything else that might be difficult for someone to cope with. Whatever the case may be, the root of the problem has to be explored at this point to understand what someone is thinking and how those thoughts are produced.

This process is often a little more challenging. It is hard to determine where the process of exploring one's thoughts begins and where it ends. By knowing how those thoughts are happening and what is causing them to evolve and change, it becomes easier for a person to have more control over one's life. When a person goes through CBT long enough, they start to notice trends and patterns in one's thoughts. These patterns might relate to what one might be thinking or how positive someone might be over certain actions or events in life.

The strategies might entail recording all the emotions or changes that someone is going through at a particular time. There has to be a sense of openness throughout the assessment process. A person who is being analyzed must be willing to have their emotional needs explored to assist in recognizing the needs that someone has and in deciding what can be done to resolve certain mental problems.

Awareness Is Vital

The next point to look at entails how well a person can be aware of the things that can come about in one's life. A patient in a CBT process has to be aware of the problems one is struggling with. This includes looking into what feelings someone might have surrounding certain concepts or ideas. These feelings might be unrealistic or caused by some difficult situation. A person's train of thought should be explored and whether it might be derailed by certain emotions. The problems that someone encounters might be a threat to their well-being.

The biggest problem with this point is that it is impossible to figure out how long it will take to have more control over one's life. There is no way to tell when a period of awareness begins and when it ends. As the emotions and thoughts are observed, a person will start to realize some of the problems one is entering into or any fallacies that might come along. Sometimes this might require a second person to help point out certain problems. These include issues like when a person is associating something with a negative concept.

The best part of the awareness stage is that the person who needs help the most will finally recognize just what is needed for success. It is through this newfound knowledge that a person will start to work toward changing one's life around and fixing the emotional worries that one has developed. Having more control over one's mind at this point is vital for the success of the task at hand.

Review Negative Things

As one becomes more aware of the feelings and emotions one has, it becomes clear that there are both positive and negative feelings and triggers that cause these feelings. As difficult as it might be for people to think about, the negative things that someone is thinking have to be explored and reviewed with care. By identifying the negative thoughts one has, it becomes easier to identify the problems that are causing the negative or harsh thoughts. Negative behavioral responses, physical issues, and other worries can make things harder for some to handle. The responses that one puts into certain concepts or ideas have to be explored in the process. The good thing about this stage is that sometimes the negative feelings might be irrational and the owner of those feelings can learn how to control them in some fashion.

Reshaping Thoughts

It is not always easy for people to think about those negative things and situations but the associated feelings have to be explored, reshaped, and adjusted. The most important step in CBT is discovering the negative thoughts or attitudes one has while finding ways to adjust them. Sometimes these issues may be adjusted by finding what is inaccurate or false and finding the truth behind certain ideas. In other cases, a person might need to be exposed to a situation or event more often. The simple work that goes into handling one's emotions and attitudes is vital to managing one's mind and keeping certain issues from being a dramatic threat to life.

An Example

To get an idea of how this entire routine works, it helps to look at an example. Let's say that Mark is trying to manage his general anxiety associated with his working life. He might have a significant mental hang-up where he constantly gets nervous when he sees that his mobile phone has a text alert. He might be afraid that the person who is contacting him might be angry. He would say that he is worried that the text alert would be from his employer. He says this because there have been many times in the past where his employer has sent angry text messages about how he is not doing his job right. Mark would become nervous when he sees that little icon on his phone telling him that something is on his phone, but in most cases, that text is not what he thinks it would be. Rather, it might be a message from someone else or a positive message from his employer.

Mark would utilize CBT to help him control and relieve his anxiety so he will not feel this way when he looks at his phone and sees that marker. In this situation, he would have to do the following:

1. Mark must assess his worry about the phone signal. He has to discuss the problem with someone who can help him.

2. He then has to establish an alliance with the person who wants to help. The alliance should be of comfort and support to him. The alliance may be with a professional therapist, although sometimes working alongside a good friend can be just as effective.

3. The anxiety must be explored in detail. The thoughts can be analyzed based on how well they have formed and what causes them to form. A review of prior events from the past may be investigated.

4. Mark must be made aware of what he is thinking. Sometimes his mind might be clouded so that he does not understand what he is doing, thus causing him to act irrationally in some cases. As Mark becomes aware, he feels a sudden need to resolve the problems.

5. This leads to a review of the negative feelings he has. Everything that he was aware of must be explored based on how positive the situation might be.

6. The reshaping process can begin at this juncture. Mark will work with a professional to help him reshape his thoughts and find new ways to control his anxiety. This includes learning how to avoid the worried feelings that he develops when he sees that text notification. He may also learn how to replace those worried thoughts or how to engage in actions that correct some of the deficiencies in his thought processes.

As Mark follows these recommendations, he will have more control over his life and how he is going to lead it. He will start to notice that there is no reason for his anxiety over that message. If anything, the alerts he gets will almost certainly be harmless or at least constructive or productive. Having the help that he needs will ensure that he can keep from being frustrated or worried about the smallest things that he encounters. It is a person's ability to handle thoughts and feelings through CBT that a person's life can improve and become healthier or easier for a person to manage.

Chapter 4 – The Value of Memory

One aspect of CBT and cognitive psychology that cannot be ignored is how memory makes an impact on one's life. It is memories that determine the thoughts and values that people hold in their daily lives. People often report that they recall things that happened when they were children. The specific memories that people have can be vague or specific. Some memories can be rather vivid and realistic.

Memories make it easier for people to have the fullest lives possible:

1. Some people might use their memories to feel motivated by the things they do.

Many people are encouraged to work harder in their lives or to live them to the fullest by recalling many things in the past. For instance, a professional basketball player might have won a major championship and has great memories of the ceremonies, parties, media appearances, and other things that came with within that huge honor. He may be motivated to keep competing and to win that title again so he can get back to all the fun things that came with his success. Perhaps he might also be motivated by memories of people saying that he wasn't going to amount to much as a basketball player.

2. People may also feel happier about themselves then they consider their memories.

It is through the memories that people can feel happy and pleased with their lives. The positive memories that people can develop include memories of their travels, their encounters with other people, and so forth.

3. Others might use memories to recall information for test or work purposes.

For instance, a college student might use memories of classes and books for a course to do well on certain assignments. That student would be more likely to succeed if he or she had a good memory that recalls the information found in their study books. A person in a work environment might use memories of an orientation or instructional session to understand what to do on the job. By recalling the memories gathered during a learning session, it becomes easier for someone to stay proficient and effective while on the job.

4. Memories are needed for effective communication.

People can use their memories to recall the people that they wish to talk with or to know how they can contact them. Being able to remember conversations or instructions is essential for communication with others in a work environment. The most important part of memory for CBT is that it is a point about one's life that might dictate what someone thinks and feels. A person's memories will form judgments based on certain attitudes or ideas that one might hold. Sometimes memories might become too difficult to manage if they are very negative. It is through those memories that it might be a challenge for someone to gain more control and use those negative memories in a positive way.

Working Memory

Cognitive psychology suggests that people have two forms of memory. The first is the working memory. Working memory focuses on the short-term things that people are thinking about and need to know at the moment, such as:

1. Sensations are produced in the brain. These sensations may come from the various things that someone might notice at the present time.

2. After paying attention to something, the sensations produced will go into one's working memory.

3. The person will analyze the memory based on the episode that is produced.

Sometimes the episode may be a one-off occasion. In other cases, this may be the first of many times that the memory in question will be used. It is easy for the working memory to be converted into one's long-term memory depending on how intense or repetitive the situation is.

4. An episodic buffer may relate the things that are taking place based on the certain functions that might occur in one's mind.

5. The working memory is compared with the long-term memory that one has.

It is easier for the working memory to be improved upon when it relates to the long-term memory one holds. This process helps manage the working memory that one wishes to use. This form of memory is not going to last very long.

How Long Does Working Memory Last?

All people have their own abilities to handle working memory. Some people can keep their working memory intact for about 30 to 90 minutes at a time. The number of things that can be stored in one's working memory can also be limited. People might store about five to ten things at a time in their working memory. These memories might entail things such as what has to be picked up or what needs to complete in an afternoon.

It is very easy for that working memory to be disrupted. The changes in one's memory might come about due to decay or interference.

Decay or Interference?

The working memory that one has will wear out after a period of time. While there are times when the working memory can be converted into a long-term memory, it is often easier for working memories to be lost. There are two reasons why this memory might disappear:

1. Decay occurs as the memory is lost over time.

Sometimes a stimulus that causes a person to become afraid or worried could cause a memory to be forgotten. This occurs through what is known as decay. As time passes, the information becomes harder for a person to recall. The memory is lost as the information becomes hard or impossible to retrieve. The information is not as accessible as it was when the memory was first produced. The brain starts to develop a trace of a memory when something comes happens, but the neurochemicals that the brain produces will be lost after a while.

Here's an example. George might be studying for a test, but he has not been able to study as well as he had hoped. He might be interrupted by other tasks relating to his studies and personal life. As a result, it becomes difficult for him to spend extra time with the subject matter. Whatever he has read will be forgotten as the stimuli needed for recalling that information is no longer available. The memories that George has about his studies will suffer from decay. As a result, it becomes harder for him to remember what he had studied. He would struggle with his test as a result of this.

George could have avoided decay by rehearsing the information he was studying. He could have spent extra time and more frequent sessions with what he was learning while also linking that content to his long-term memory. By doing this, it becomes easier for him to recall the things that he was learning. This, in turn, would make it easier for him to succeed on his test.

   2. Interference makes it harder for the brain to think about things.

Interference is another problem that can influence one's memory. Interference occurs when other memories interfere with each other, thus making it harder for certain ideas of thoughts to come forward in one's mind. For George, he might have dealt with many memories or feelings entering his mind while studying. He might have done well with rehearsing his information to store it in his long-term memory. After a while, it might become harder for him to manage all those memories. He might struggle to keep the memories intact as he starts to think about what might happen during the test. Maybe something relating to a long-term memory from another course could get in the way.

This does contribute to memory decay in a sense. It might get to the point where something someone has been trying to remember is quickly forgotten because the mind is focused on something else.

The best way to explain this would be to compare it with what might happen when someone is trying to complete a certain task in a working environment. That person could be swamped with tasks and will forget about a certain thing that has to be done. This will end up being complicated and in many cases unintentional, but it is through that interference that one's working memory can be lost. In George's case, it could be because he had several new tasks develop while he was studying for his test; those new tasks could have made him forget what he was supposed to be doing.

The working memory concentrates on understanding the sudden triggers that a person may encounter. When a person starts to struggle, it becomes harder for them to feel confident or comfortable with certain aspects relating to life. Knowing how the working memory can change and evolve is critical to recognizing what issues someone might have and how those problems can be resolved regarding managing one's mental risks or issues.

Long-Term Memory

The second type of memory covered in cognitive psychology is a long-term memory. As the name suggests, this refers to something that a person has stored in one's mind for a longer period of time. Long-term memory is important to consider when it comes to fears. The things that people recall the most from the past are things that could result in being a dramatic burden. Sometimes the intense memories that someone has of a traumatic event or something else negative in nature might make it harder for a person to feel confident and comfortable with one's life. That difficult memory can disturb one's concentration and make it difficult to feel good about what they are trying to do with their lives. It is through one's long-term memory that negative feelings and thoughts might persist.

For a memory to become a long-term memory, it has to be stored. This is regardless of whether the memory was from a few years back or if it just happened in the past hour. Long-term memory can still be affected by decay or interference.

Some details might be forgotten, or new memories might push the old ones out of the way or at least make them a little harder for people to recall. Long-term memory can be years at a time or a few weeks or months depending on the issue.

Procedural Memory

There are three types of long-term memory in cognitive psychology. The first is a procedural memory. This is a type of memory that focuses on certain actions or procedures that a person engages in, hence the name. Procedural memory often entails routine tasks that someone might engage in regularly. A person might use one's procedural memory to recall the directions to drive from one place to another. Another person may use that memory to recall how to prepare a recipe for dinner.

Procedural memories can settle into the brain quickly. It is through the repetition of certain tasks that these memories are made and become difficult to eliminate. Procedural memory can be used to manage fear or anxiety as people can use certain procedures to keep their minds under control and calm. Procedural memory is not emotional. The daily procedures might be regular or comforting.

Semantic Memory

The other two types of long-term memory to use are declarative memories – semantic and episodic. This refers to some of the events that someone encounters. Semantic memory involves one's knowledge of certain events or concepts in life. This includes memories of factual information and events that have taken place in the past. People can declare their semantic memories to other people as needed.

The specific things covered in semantic memories involve factual information:

- Words and their meanings are included in semantic memories. This includes how to pronounce those words and know the synonyms and antonyms of those words.

- Concepts relating to certain facts are included in one's semantic memory. These concepts focus on what someone has learned or read in a book or magazine or viewed online or through a television program.

- General trivial knowledge counts as semantic memory as well. People might learn interesting tidbits over time and eventually move them in the back of their minds. Sometimes the factual points might be more unique than usual.

Semantic memories relate to psychology in that they are what people think they know about certain items. A person who is afraid of flying in a plane might have a semantic memory that includes details on famous aviation disasters and stories about things that could go wrong while flying in a plane. With proper conditioning, a person's semantic memory can be improved to focus on the good things about planes and how they are so much safer today than in the past.

Episodic Memory

Episodic memory is the personal things that someone does. This part of declarative memory includes the things that a person has memories about, such as:

- Things that happened at school or at work. This includes the memory of schedules, daily activities, any tests one took, or any presentations that were given.

- Romantic memories include situations such as when someone met his or her romantic partner for the first time or when they got married or engaged. Details on the things someone might have done while on dates or other romantic events might be included.

- Travel memories may be included - details on the places visited, the events attended, any hotels and dining spots, and so forth.

Episodic memories can be reviewed when understanding what causes a person to become depressed or to suffer from substantial grief in life. Sometimes these memories might be embedded deep in one's mind and could be harder to access. Those difficult memories are known as repressed memories. They are memories that a person has not released out in the open and in many cases are ones that have not necessarily been thought about much. These memories will have persisted in the back of one's mind and are waiting to be accessed eventually.

Episodic memories may also trigger anxiety or fear. A single event in one's memory could be responsible for triggering feelings of fear that is hard to understand. The most intriguing part of the episodic memory is that it moves deeper in the conscious mind than any other type of memory. The conscious mind will be more likely to store the episodic memory better than other memories because they are the things that someone has directly been in touch with.

The greatest problem surrounding the episodic memories is that some people might put more weight on some of these memories than others. People often try to put more weight on the positive ones. They will do this by looking back at the details they can recall while thinking about the good things that have happened. Negative episodic memories are always likely to become stronger. The disturbing triggers or situations that someone encounters, in this case, might make for a dramatic threat to a person's life.

Is Long-Term Memory More Important Than Working Memory?

It is through long-term memory that it is easier for a person to feel happy and positive while producing more good memories throughout one's life. It is very important to have this memory to be intact to have a successful life. People should not take the working memory lightly. With a strong working memory, a person can handle a variety of functions and actions, to handle certain tasks based on the chores one needs to finish, how many details are involved, and in what order they need to be done.

Neurons and Their Impact on Memory

Neurons are nerve cells formed within the brain. They produce signals through each other via natural electrical impulses known as electrochemical signaling. Neurons are not going to divide, nor are they going to die and eventually be replaced by new ones. As neurons develop and function, they help send signals that reach many parts of the brain. These include parts that store memories and keep them intact so that people have healthy memories that develop appropriately. When more neurons are active, it becomes easier for the brain to produce the memories one needs. The memories will be easier to store and utilize throughout one's life when enough neurons work in the process.

Unfamiliarity Is Vital

The regular procedures and work routines that people do each day are not going to be all that outstanding or unique in one's memory. A person who has been working at the same place for the past fifteen years probably does not recall an individual day at the office from three years ago, let alone one from a week ago. The familiarity of the situation keeps a person from being likely to think about anything that is unique or intriguing about the situation in question. When something is unfamiliar, it becomes easy for the brain to change its ways of thinking. A person might notice after a while that something unique or interesting could be worth paying more attention to.

This is a good reason why memories of vacations are so vivid and easy to recall. A trip to some new place will create intense memories of new sights, sounds, and experiences. The brain's neurons will be more active as they create new connections and memories. It is through this that the experiences of going to someplace special are surely more interesting than what one experiences in daily life. A negative memory might also be easier for the brain to store. This is especially true for some negative event that might be more intense than what one might be comfortable with.

Are Negative Issues Stronger?

A good explanation of why negative memories are likely to be stronger and more pervasive is due to how people might feel more stress in their brains during those events. There is a chance that more neurons will start to function and become more active while a person feels emotional from a traumatic event. This makes it easier for those events to be recalled with ease. The brain functions might be strong enough so that the feelings of an event can be cataloged and recalled quickly. For instance, a person who is in a car wreck might develop intense and vivid memories of that wreck due to the brain becoming so active. As the brain is active, a person will feel uncomfortable and feel intense stress and pressure due to the accident. All that stress makes the brain more active. This, in turn, creates more intense memories.

Childhood

A person's brain can work overtime to produce feelings that one might not be all that familiar with. It is in childhood that it is easier for these neurons to work. The growing and evolving brain will continue to produce neurons to help secure the memories that one wishes to save. The most important part of managing neurons during adolescence is that they help to generate the memories one wishes to utilize well into the future. The memories produced in one's childhood will be easier to secure into one's long-term memory. As the neurons grow and move with greater efficiency, it becomes easier for the neurons to secure experiences one has at a young age into one's memory.

This is vital when it comes to fears and how they are produced. Commonplace fears stay in the mind because they will have developed those fears very early in one's life. This could make it harder for the child to function without being afraid of certain concepts that the child encounters later in life.

What Are the Oldest Memories?

It is easy for many of the earliest memories someone has to be lost over time. A parent might ask a child if they remember something that happened a few years back, and they might have no real recollection of it. Perhaps it could be because they were not fully conscious of the world around them at the time.

It might also be because those children were too busy with learning other new things.

Many people will lose details on what they recalled when they were seven years of age or younger. These memories are lost due to what is known as childhood amnesia. In this case, a person will stop remembering some of the things that happened while growing up. This does not mean that certain memories that one has of their childhood will be lost. The problem is that many fragments of those memories will be recalled, but not all of them will persist.

For instance, an adult might recall a few things relating to growing up and watching television on Saturday mornings when they were eight or nine years of age. An adult might recall waking up, pouring a bowl of cereal, going into the next room to watch television, and enjoying shows. Some specific memories might be recalled. A person might recall the specific cereal or certain details about keeping the sound down to keep from waking parents or getting up early enough to watch the television station sign on for the day.

However, childhood amnesia is when not all of these memories will be recalled. The person might not remember many details about the room that they watched television in. They might not even recall any of the specific programs that they watched. Every person's memory develops in different ways. By working with a stronger and more capable memory, it becomes easier for someone to recall more details about what they might have done in the past. Regardless of how memory develops, the things that one recalls must be used as a key part of cognitive psychology. Understanding the memories that a person has, how they were formed, and how long those feelings have persisted could make an impact on whatever one wishes to do.

Chapter 5 – Metacognition

Metacognition is a part of psychology and CBT that focuses on personal thoughts. Sometimes cognitive psychology goes beyond just what someone is thinking. This study can also delve into what people think about their thoughts through self-reflection. It becomes easier to identify the source of what someone might be thinking through metacognition. The feelings that a person has about those thoughts could also show how motivated a person is to make a change in one's life and to stop thinking about certain things that could become harmful.

The feelings someone has during the CBT process can happen when someone thinks about the emotions being experienced. For instance, Janet might be depressed as a result of how she has not done as much with her life as other people. While she might be depressed, Janet might feel upset with those thoughts. She wants to eliminate that depression. She might hate the feelings that she has because she is constantly being subjected to troubling worries that make it harder for her to feel better about what she is doing with her life. Janet would enter into CBT as a means of resolving her depression. The feelings she has toward her depression would cause her to want to resolve the issue. Through further CBT and analysis, she will discover precisely what is happening and why she has certain feelings about her emotions.

About Metacognition

Metacognition focuses on how well memories and thoughts are produced. Those who generate their own values about their feelings or emotions will start to notice many things that should still be explored with careful consideration and thought. There are many aspects of metacognition that can be explored. These considerations all relate to cognitive psychology as they focus on people recognizing their feelings.

The Three Main Types of Knowledge

Metacognition can be divided up into three types of knowledge.

1. Declarative Knowledge

Declarative knowledge focuses on what one knows about certain things and knowing certain facts. For instance, Robin might be working hard in his tool shed to fix his car. He could hold declarative knowledge relating to the parts of his car has and what he needs to do to fix what needs to be fixed.

2. Procedural Knowledge

Procedural knowledge is knowing about doing certain things. This might be following certain steps to do certain procedures and actions. In this case, Robin might understand the many procedures that have to be followed. Robin will look at things like the steps needed to change the oil in his vehicle or how to repair the suspension. His ability to understand many procedures will help him get the most out of the work he wishes to put in.

3. Conditional Knowledge

Conditional knowledge involves knowing when to use a procedure or when to use one's knowledge. Robin would use his conditional knowledge to identify when his car needs an oil change, for instance. Each of these three types of knowledge combines in metacognition to recognize what people can do when they encounter many situations. People might have a better understanding of what they can do based on not only certain behaviors or actions but also through the attitudes one holds.

Déjà Vu

One of the most common considerations about metacognition is the sensation that someone has experienced something before. This phenomenon is known as déjà vu. When a person experiences déjà vu, they have a feeling that they have been in a certain situation before. It is about familiarity and knowing that there's something going on that might be reminiscent of an occurrence in the past. Déjà vu is not likely to occur in situations where the event took place recently. People often recognize déjà vu when certain things about an event start popping up in their minds out of nowhere. The sudden memories those people develop will become strong.

There are many reasons why someone might experience déjà vu:

1. A person has a strong memory.
2. Someone might have had a dream involving a certain situation.
3. A person has heard something in the past but is not fully aware of what it might be.

The concept of deja entendu is where a person is sure they have felt or heard something in the past. Many people who have concerns surrounding fear or anxiety often experience déjà vu when they get into situations that are troubling to them. They begin to feel as though an experience right now might relate to another experience they had in the past. This creates a sense of fear or worry. CBT helps to analyze when déjà vu occurs and what might make a situation in one's life harder to manage. Knowing what might be happening in one's life can be dramatic and vital to understand and recognize.

Déjà vu unravels some of the mysteries that surround the mind. Many of the memories that someone has might be hidden in the back of the mind because the mind is too busy focused on newer ideas. The second experience in one situation may result in a person suddenly revealing past memories. By working with déjà vu in the exploration and awareness processes, people can have their memories explored and revealed in ways they might have never imagined they could be.

Cryptomnesia

There are times when a person might have forgotten something that took place in the past, but eventually, the memory returns. If the person does not recognize the memory as something that happened in the past and is seen as a new or original concept that has never happened before, this phenomenon is known as cryptomnesia.

For instance, Sam might suddenly start to recall a memory of something he did while on vacation in Chicago. He might begin to recall when he went out to one of the beaches on the city's lakeside. Sam might think that this memory is new. He starts to recall that memory as if it were a new experience. In this case, he does not recall that he actually had this experience. The sudden recollection that he develops out of that memory is random in nature, but it is a point that will directly influence what he thinks or does. In Sam's case, he suddenly notices that she went out to a beach near Chicago and thinks that he was doing this for the first time in his life. However, in reality, he completely forgot about this experience or did not have an understanding of this concept in his mind. This led to changing his thoughts and attitudes over what she wanted to do.

An even better example of this is a historical example of cryptoamnesia. When the philosopher Friedrich Nietzsche wrote his novel Thus Spoke Zarathustra, he wrote about a certain event that was published in a book more than fifty years prior. Nietzsche's recollection of the event was accurate, but there was the controversy that he could have plagiarized the content.

Nietzsche was dealing with cryptomnesia when producing this part of his book. He had read the book when he was younger. He might have come up with the event with the belief that it was something that never took place before, but in reality, he had actually read about it in the past and noticed some details. Therefore, this originated from something that he remembered from the past and not from trying to intentionally copy an experience someone else had.

Cryptoamnesia is a concept where someone will have done or experienced an event and will eventually recall it while thinking it was a new event. Whether it is Sam recalling going to a beach as though it was something new to her mind or Nietzsche remembering something that he read years after he last consciously knew it, this is a point about metacognition that can influence what one might think. Cryptoamnesia may also relate to repressed memories. That is, it could be something that a person has recalled, but they are not fully aware of what might be going on. The sudden worries or concerns a person might develop can prove to be a challenge in some of the most difficult cases.

Imagination Inflation

Sometimes the things someone thinks about can prove to be difficult to live with. A person might develop new thoughts that might be perceived as being true even if they were never events that actually took place. A person's imagination can become exaggerated. In this case, a person might struggle with imagination inflation. This is a problem where a person is imagining a memory that took place in the past, but that event never actually happened. The imagination inflation process involves a person becoming increasingly confident and certain that the event took place.

This aspect of cognitive psychology focuses on how people might change some of the things they experience and think about. Those who experience imagination inflation will start to feel that something is real even when they never took place, to begin with. People might become convinced after a while they experienced something when they hadn't, thus making them want to act upon what they have explored.

An example of this can be found in the false confession. This is a point in criminal justice that is caused by a person coerced into admitting wrongdoings or someone takes advantage of a person's mental illness. A police officer will interrogate a suspect and have that person imagine the crime taking place. This may eventually lead to a suspect feeling that they actually committed the crime even though it never took place. Although it is considered to be an unethical practice, it is a concern that can directly influence what a suspect believes to be true.

Imagination inflation is a problem that directly relates to how well a person is capable of remembering things. If a person is told several times over that something actually did happen, that someone might be encouraged to believe that the event in question is indeed true. The most essential part of imagination inflation is that the memories produced in this situation have to be intense and vivid. It is through the strong visualization that a person might begin to think that something fictional was real.

Validity Effect

The validity effect occurs when:

1. A person will not believe in a certain statement.

2. The statement is repeated many times over. This could be repeated regularly over the course of days or weeks.

3. After a while, the person who did not believe a statement at first will start to believe that the statement is true.

Even the greatest falsehoods could be interpreted as being true if the information is repeated often enough and is convincing to the audience.

A good way to explain this can come from the political campaigns that people around the world often engage in. Politicians can produce sound bites and statements that are in their favor or are intended to harm the other party. If that politician is assertive and keeps repeating a certain argument, the audience will begin to believe that it is true.

This is a concern that may influence how a person might feel about fears. Many fears develop because people are persistent in thinking about what they believe through the validity effect. For instance, a person who is afraid of dogs might be fearful because they have heard or seen several times that dogs can be dangerous. This is in spite of evidence to the contrary. Identifying the validity effect is important to note when looking at how to manage a person's mental stability. There will be a need to provide a person with correct information and enough sources to get that someone to realize that the false beliefs they have fallen for are not accurate. The validity effect may relate to the concept of imagination inflation as well. The validity effect will cause a person to believe that something happened in the past when it didn't.

False Fame Effect

The false fame effect concentrates on some of the more interesting things that can develop in one's life. It is through the false fame effect that whatever might not be famous or recognizable is immediately easy for a person to recognize. Here's an example of how the false fame effect works. A person might be attending a minor league baseball game where they will notice the players on the team are aiming to make it to a major league roster where they will play with the best players and earn the most recognition and money. The person attending the game might look through the roster and recognize a person's name. After finding additional information on the player, it turns out that the player in question is not actually a person that one remembers. Instead, they just think that the name sounds familiar.

This is an example of the false fame effect. A person will recognize something and think that it is more recognizable than what it is really like. This point might be linked to fears in some way in that a person's false fame effects might be certain emotions that are too hard to live, but they are ones that might be brought up based on prior memories one might have. Those memories could be rather intense depending on what someone is handling at a time, but they are concerns that should be explored.

How Well Are Concepts Managed in Metacognition?

There are three parts of metacognition that may be explored in detail. These points focus mainly on how well certain beliefs might occur when recognizing one's feelings. Having a clear idea of what one's beliefs or feelings are is vital to the CBT process, but it is through these three points that people have to explore to make the most out of their metacognition efforts:

1. Planning

Concepts in the mind are organized through planning. This is where the human mind analyzes the strategies and resources that one will use to manage certain ideas responsibly. The resources have to be allocated well enough to make it easier for tasks to be handled. In metacognition, a person might plan to do something like go to a grocery store or to plan a vacation. The planning must be arranged responsibly.

2. Monitoring

Monitoring is a process where a person becomes aware of the things that someone is doing when trying to manage ideas or concepts in one's mind. A person has to monitor one's performance during any task. In CBT, monitoring focuses on how well a person can identify how certain emotions are occurring and how intense they might be.

3. Evaluating

After a while, a person has to start evaluating one's work and efforts. The evaluation process in metacognition requires a person to look at how well the procedure was handled. Whatever was planned will be implemented and then monitored, thus leading to the evaluation stage. Evaluations can take as long as needed, but they must all have the same goals. These include goals such as a desire to plan one's mental functions carefully and a need to discover the roots of certain thoughts In order to manage one's emotions and thoughts. The goal is to look at how well a person completed a task and if that person was successful in their efforts at being a better or more productive person in society.

Introspection Is Key

The most important thing to consider regarding one's work in metacognition is introspection. It is through introspection that it becomes easier for a person to manage one's thoughts. Introspection is about working with an understanding of one's thoughts. Part of this includes finding a new sense of awareness about what someone might be doing and how those ideas might develop. Having a better sense of introspection is critical for one's life.

Introspection requires people to look into the feelings they have and analyze them to see how well they are organized. The goal is to fully understand what is causing someone to feel a certain way. Having a good plan for managing one's introspective attitudes is critical for handling one's life without any problems over what one wants to do in life. It takes a bit of time for people to be fully introspective. Those who can handle the process of being introspective will be capable of recognizing more than just what they have done or what they have felt. They will understand that everything they have done in a day had some kind of reason or purpose to it. The hard work and strong effort they put into their lives will have been worthwhile thanks to how they have focused on what they are doing in their lives. Those who do better with introspective thoughts will be more likely to feel comfortable about what they are doing and how they are leading their life.

It is through introspection that a person will feel confident or comfortable with the attitudes one holds.

An Emphasis on Realism

The most important part of introspection entails the realism that comes along. The effort must look into not only the memories themselves but also what could have caused them to develop. A review of events and experiences in one's life are vital to figuring out what is causing someone to think and feel in some fashion. Sometimes the introspection will not come across anything that could be a root of the issue. The patient must consider the threats of false fame, validity, and inflation when seeing what someone might be thinking. It is through these problems that someone might struggle to come across the right thoughts or values when trying to manage one's emotions or attitudes.

When there are no background details about one's thoughts, there exists the chance that the person might be experiencing some imaginary beliefs. It is up to the person to realize that what someone was thinking or being influenced by is fictional and should not be taken seriously.

How Are Sparks of Interest Formed?

An intriguing aspect of metacognition also involves some of the cases in which a person might experience dramatic changes in one's feelings. A spark of interest might develop quickly in just a few moments. A spark of interest occurs when a person suddenly feels interested in something. For instance, a spark of interest might occur when someone hears or sees something interesting or worthwhile. There is always a chance that a spark of interest will get someone to pay attention to something that might be fascinating and worth exploring.

For instance, a spark of interest might form as a result of a person hearing something funny or amusing. The spark only takes a few moments to start up, but it can be very intense. This is a fascinating aspect of cognitive psychology that will quickly influence one's thoughts. Here's an example of a spark of interest. Tom might be interested in cooking, but he is also afraid of hurting himself while cooking. As a result, he might avoid using sharp knives while cooking. He wants to keep the utensils he uses for cooking secure while being easy to use.

He might develop a spark of interest when he hears a story relating to cooking and new developments in that field. Such a story might be a new series of utensils he could use for taking care of various cooking tasks. Tom might take a strong interest in what is being highlighted and how well certain things can be used in his life. It is through that spark of interest that he will pay more attention. The most impressive part of the spark of interest one might develop is that there is no way to tell when such a spark is going to happen.

Metacognition is a valuable part of cognitive psychology and CBT that has to be explored. People have to look carefully at how their thoughts develop and what they can do with them. It is through metacognition that a person might have an easier time managing various functions and actions in life.

Chapter 6 – The Importance of Perception

People will come into contact with various stimuli in their daily lives. They will see unique things, smell intriguing scents, taste various foods, and hear sounds in their homes and outside. It is through a person's perception that things can be identified. The basic definition of perception is that it is the act of noticing what is in the environment. While perception is often associated with the physical things that someone might experience, this concept is more than that. Perception is also about how people interpret certain concepts.

Here's a brief example of how someone might perceive things:

1. A car is rolling along the street. One person might say, "Look at that car going down the road."

2. The second person might be more specific and perceive something extra about the vehicle. That someone would say, "Look at that blue car moving along the road."

3. A third person might be even more perceptive, looking at some of the specific features that can be found on that car. The person might see that the vehicle is not only a car but also a fancy BMW sports car. The third person would say, "Look at that new blue BMW going down the road."

The third person is the most perceptive person in this case. While the first two people are noticing the basic things about the car, the third notices the specific type of car and that it is made by a certain auto company. That third person might have noticed something interesting surrounding that car. So, what does perception have to do with CBT? It is through the perception that a person is able to identify what someone might feel. It is the detail of what is causing someone to be afraid or worried about something. The art of perception is important to recognize. With CBT, people have to perceive the issues that have caused them to act in certain ways. They need to notice what they are doing and why their lives have changed because of certain problems in their lives.

Interpretation

The key part of perception for cognitive therapy involves the processes used to determine what a person might be doing or experiencing. Everyone has the power to observe things in many ways based on their senses of sight, taste, hearing, and so forth. Everyone has their own interests that determine what they perceive. Some people might perceive the songs of birds and can identify each species if that is what they are interested in. Another person might only be able to perceive that they hear a songbird but have not the idea of the species of bird, nor do they care because it is not what interests them.

There are often times when a person might be inspired to follow certain ideas based on the things one sees and how someone interprets it.

Structuralism

One aspect relating to cognitive thought is structuralism. This is a field that focuses on how people perceive certain ideas or values. Structuralism is a practice that focuses on what people might review while in a general state of consciousness. The simplest concepts may be used to identify what someone is thinking or feeling. Although it is not used as often as other theories, structuralism may still be used to understand how people interpret things and events.

The goal of structuralism is to review a person's consciousness and how it is changing and evolving. For instance, a person might be presented with a certain item or stimulus. They are asked to describe what it is like. The words and feelings that are evoked by the stimulus can be used to understand what that person might be thinking or feeling. The sensations that a person feels while noticing something may also be explored in the practice. These sensations often occur when someone looks at an item and has something to say about their feeling surrounding the item in question.

A person could be presented with different items and asked to answer certain questions based on their feelings about an item. Knowing how to express one's values or ideas about what they see can indicate underlying values and biases. Structuralism is not very popular today but could be used to understand how a person might feel about one sensory item versus another. It could help determine the images or ideas that a person can use when trying to replace negative thoughts. For instance, a fearful sensory item that relates to one concept or event may be swapped in favor of a different one that is positive.

Why Perception?

Although the things that may be used when working with perception in cognitive behavioral therapy can be diverse, it is important to use this to get clues as to what someone might be feeling. On the surface, a person's fears or other worries may be confirmed through perception. Those fears and concerns may also be confirmed based on how a person might respond to certain problems. Knowing how perception works is critical to understand what someone fears and respects versus what someone might be comfortable with. The use of perception gives people an idea of what to expect when dealing with others in most situations. Perception in cognitive behavioral therapy focuses on what people can do to grow and thrive by understanding what they are doing and why.

Chapter 7 – Using CBT to Handle One's Perception

The goal of CBT is to recognize what one might notice in a situation and how intense or minor it might be. The biggest goal of CBT is to get an appropriate perspective for the perceptions one has. This chapter concentrates on the use of CBT to manage one's perception and how things might be noticed on a daily basis so that a person's mind might be better organized.

Identifying Self-Image Issues

How a person perceives oneself is the first thing to understand. This should focus on identifying what problems one has that can result in false conclusions.

Several things can be done:

1. Think about the values that one has. These include values about personal attitudes.

For instance, CBT may work to identify some of the things that one is doing. Someone might have an idea that they are not good at something and therefore will never be good at it.

2. Take a piece of paper and write down ten strengths.

Strengths can be anything someone is good at. The key is to focus on things that one perceives is worthwhile.

3. Write ten weaknesses on the same paper.

The weaknesses can be minor or significant. The person engaging in this test should be as honest about those weaknesses as possible so the CBT process can continue.

4. Analyze the two lines and decide how realistic these are while planning what can be done to manage the weaknesses.

This point in CBT focuses on helping a person recognize some of the problems that have developed and what can be done to resolve these issues. The positives can be explored to see what they can do to help fix the negatives. An even better idea is to look at the intensity of the positives versus how extreme the negatives are. Doing so makes it easier for people who are depressed about their lives to stay in check. False conclusions often make it harder for people to handle their lives. It is important to notice some of the things that could be a real concern.

Seek Outside Help

It never hurts to get a bit of outside help to get answers about what one needs to do and how certain problems can be resolved. Outside help is getting a second opinion to help determine how to correct issues one has encountered.

The steps to find outside help:

1. Talk with a trustworthy friend or professional.

This relates to the alliance person of managing CBT. An alliance must be produced between the person seeking help and someone they view as trustworthy. Sometimes this might be a professional psychologist who can help, but in many cases talking with a friend might be good enough. A person could choose to talk over issues with another person in the family, a good friend that one regularly talks to, or a fellow classmate or co-worker with whom they have good relations and trust.

2. Talk with that person and ask for a direct opinion.

Be specific about asking for help or an opinion. The truth hurts at times, but it is through the truth that it becomes easier for people to correct situations. Do not assume that anyone who claims to be direct and honest is going to be truthful. Often there might be occasions in which a person might be too afraid to deliver an accurate and true opinion about something.

3. Read between the lines.

Sometimes a person might not be fully honest. They might try to hide certain feelings or statements out of fear. That is, a person is afraid of what might happen if he or she says something that might be interpreted as being harsh or hard to accept. Pay attention to what someone didn't say. Did the person actually hear the question? Was someone hesitant to answer a question? Maybe they danced around their words to try to create a softer response. Sometimes a person might be slow to respond. Such a case is a sign that someone is afraid to tell the truth for fear of hurting the person. It is often a challenge to make a negative statement even if it is not what the other wants to hear.

4. Keep talking with that person. Express a warm feeling and a sense of acceptance.

Be calm around the other person and express a sense of gratitude. By showing a warm feeling, it becomes easier for the truth to be shared. Respecting the truth makes a difference when trying to resolve the emotional problems or fears one has. By explaining the truth and being direct about it, the conversation will be easier. No one will fear what is being said. Instead, the people will respect the opinions and attitudes that are being expressed on all sides.

The most important part of finding outside help in this part of CBT is to not be afraid of what might happen in this situation. People often worry about asking for help at this stage because they do not want to get into any emotional or personal trouble with other people. When talking with others in the CBT process, it becomes easier for the issues one has to be explored and discussed in detail. A person should not feel stressed when hearing what someone else has to say. CBT is about bringing the truth out to the forefront. This might not always be the best thing to think or feel, but it is essential to be able to have a smart and fruitful conversation. Refusing to accept what is being said might make the situation worse. It would become harder for that other person to be willing to speak or to try and get one's point across.

Adjust Perception Based on Feedback

The feedback can be used to manage one's perception. The perception has to be changed to make it easier for someone to face their fears.

The perceptions one has should be controlled by:

- Look at what needs to improve. This is based on the weaknesses that were written earlier and the direct conversation someone had with another person.

- Analyze one's goals in life and compare them with what has to change to attain those goals.

- Identify how one's positives can be utilized to correct the negatives.

This is a well-rounded approach, and it is a part of CBT that helps manage one's mind and to keep a person from feeling depressed or unhappy. With CBT, the perception one has can be reorganized based on what one might realistically think or feel at a time. Knowing how to handle this perception the right way is crucial to maintaining a healthier life. The best way to manage the feedback is to be directly open with whoever is going to deliver the response. Everyone should be direct and open in any situation. The goal is to be transparent.

Consider the Habits of Other People

Observing how other people behave at certain times can guide one's behaviors and produce a simple approach to behavior that might make a difference in what one wishes to do. This part of CBT focuses on understanding what other people do to become successful. Observing the habits of others who are working hard to improve their lives and to be more productive always makes it easier for someone to know what to do right.

When observing other people include these points:

1. Look at how people respond to certain situations. What do they do to keep themselves calm and in control?

2. See what causes people to feel positive. Look at how much of an effort people use to change and improve upon their skills.

3. Identify how people interact with each other. The most successful people recognize that they can do more when they are open with others and willing to listen.

Observing how others use their habits is a good option to review, but it does help to think carefully about what one wishes to handle in a situation so the problem is not much of a threat. In summary, being ready to manage one's perception through CBT is vital for having a stronger life to fully understand what can be done to keep one's life in check and at ease. The work that goes into handling one's perception helps to determine the fears or anxieties one has or to see that someone can indeed make a difference in life without feeling depressed.

Chapter 8 – How Attention Works

When someone is told to pay attention, that person is being encouraged to listen and focus on something that is being presented. This requires that person to listen to whatever is going on at the moment. What is attention, and how is it relevant to cognitive psychology? Attention is another word for awareness. When a person pays attention, that person is aware of one's surroundings and actions. A person who pays attention will be capable of identifying the most important details and ideas that might be introduced. The goal of attention is to take in the details and filter them. The things that someone sees will be filtered based on what one wishes to concentrate on the most.

This point of cognitive psychology is highly relevant to many negative emotions or concerns. A person who suffers from depression might focus their attention on only their negative thoughts or feelings. Feelings of anxiety occur when people pay attention to the bad things that are happening and the worst case scenarios that someone might think they'll experience.

How This Relates to Perception

On the surface, attention sounds like the same thing as perception. Both situations entail knowing more about what is happening at any time. Attention is different in that attention focuses on something that someone wishes to note. A highly perceptive person might notice many details, but it is through one's attention that the details might be focused on just one aspect. Let's go back to the example of the car that someone might have noticed while on the road. A highly perceptive person would be able to say more about that car. Instead of just saying that the car is blue, that person would state that the car is a blue BMW sedan with a leather interior.

Attention is being able to recall very specific things about that vehicle. A person will concentrate on many things within that vehicle. The attentive person will be able to focus on the appearance of the BMW decal or even a dent or other imperfection found on the outside of the vehicle.

Some of the things a person might pay attention to include:

- The driver or the specific passengers in the vehicle
- Any slight damages or stains on the body of the vehicle
- Any bumper stickers or other decals
- The license plate number and the state

A person who pays attention will concentrate on not just everything but rather on one or two specific things. Attention is like perception only it is laser-focused.

Top-Down vs. Bottom-Up

There are two basic forms of attention. These focus mainly on the scope of what someone notices.

1. Top-Down Attention

Top-down attention is when the brain actively chooses to ignore something and instead focuses on one thing. For instance, Michael might be at a dinner event and is trying to enjoy his meal. However, there is a noisy couple at the table next to him. Michael is trying to keep from being bothered by that couple. He would use top-down attention to focus on things around him outside of that couple. He will focus on the dinner he is eating, the scenery around him, or the people at his table. He will be trying to ignore the annoying couple. He will think more about what he is enjoying and less about some couple that might be bothering him and making it hard for him to enjoy his meal.

2. Bottom-Up Attention

Bottom-up attention is when the brain is directly focusing and paying attention to something. A person will concentrate more on what someone is trying to say or something else. The brain will place its attention in a more focused way. In the case of the dinner date, Michael might use bottom-up attention to focus on the person next to him at the table. He would pay attention to what that someone is saying and respond with his own words. The key here is to let the dinner event be a more personalized affair. While there are plenty of things going on around him, Michael is focused on the people who are at his table.

Top-down attention is filtering out something one does not want to hear while bottom-up involves actively focusing on one particular thing. This is all about producing a comfortable situation where someone knows what should be focused on or what that person needs to avoid or ignore.

Visual or Auditory?

The attention that someone holds will be in a visual or auditory form. Sometimes a person is trying to look at something. In other cases, that person will focus on hearing what someone has to say. During the dinner event, Michael will switch his attention from visual to auditory and back again:

1. To start, he would use his visual attention to see where he is going to be sitting. He will notice the certain seat that will be his.

2. Second, Michael will continue to use his visual attention to notice the menu to see what is interesting and what he wants to order.

3. He then uses his visual attention to notice the people around him.

4. His auditory attention then reviews what people are saying. He will hear both the things people are saying and what they are saying to him and he will respond.

5. The visual attention takes over when he receives the meal he ordered. He would look at the meal and consider how he is going to consume the meal.

It is often easier for people to concentrate on either visual or auditory attention at a time. The attention will be stronger when the person can use both when understanding what people have to say or who is speaking.

Change Blindness

There are often times when a person's attention might not be as strong as it should be. Change blindness can occur when a person fails to notice a change in the environment around them. Change blindness can be considered to be a sizable gap in one's behavior. When a person fails to notice something, it becomes harder for that someone to be ready for whatever might happen next.

An example of change blindness could be seen on a major highway. Janet might be driving her vehicle along a highway and will be maintaining the same speed. At one point, she may be pulled over and ticketed for speeding because she had failed to pay attention to a change in the speed limit along her route due to construction. She did not pay attention to the change in her environment. Because of her change blindness, Janet did not know that she was supposed to have slowed down in this new environment.

Even those who regularly pay attention will not recognize every single change that takes place. In Janet's case, she might have noticed that the road was changing from three lanes to two, but maybe she did not notice that the speed limit changed just as well. That sudden change caused her to not slow down even though she was supposed to have done just that to be safe and within the law.

The length of time it takes for a person to experience change blindness can vary. Some people might take a few moments to notice a change. Others will be so focused on individual things in an area that the change will not be recognized at all. This problem often makes it harder for people to respond to the things they might or should notice in a situation.

Inattentive Blindness

Inattentive blindness is a problem when a person fails to notice certain objects or stimuli because their attention is elsewhere. In Janet's case, she might have had inattentive blindness because she was focusing too much on staying in the same lane while traveling the highway. She did not notice that there was a change in the speed limit because she had been too focused on staying in the right lane. Janet might have focused on the lane because she had anxiety over what could happen if she veered out of the lane. She was anxious about the potential of having a wreck, and this led her to not pay attention to other things in her environment.

Selective Attention

Selective attention is when a person focuses on a specific stimulus when multiple things are presented at once. This works well for CBT as it gives a person an idea of what might be causing someone to feel a certain emotion at a time based on what is in a space.

Selective attention works with one of many concepts:

1. The spotlight model

The spotlight model is when a person places a virtual spotlight on one specific thing without being bothered by other items. There will be some things outside of the focal point to notice and these items are in what is called the fringe, things that are close in proximity. For example, a person might be at a music festival where several bands are playing on multiple stages. During that festival, a person might want to focus on one band at a time. The stage will be the spotlight where most attention is paid. Meanwhile, the fringe would be the surroundings near that stage. The fringe can include things like the people in the crowd, the food vendors that are near, the other stages nearby, and anything else. These things will add to the scene, but they are not going to be as important to the scene as the spotlight that person has as the main focus. The area outside of the fringe is the margin. In the concert setting, the margin would be the large parking space or other areas near or bordering the event.

2. The zoom-lens model

The zoom-lens model is somewhat similar to the spotlight model in that this too focuses on a certain item in an environment. Beyond that, there is a significant difference. The person has the ability to move their attention as inward or outward as one wants. In this case, the person can move the spotlight to be as big or small as needed. This is a more flexible approach to attention that warrants a better sense of control over the things that one might be noticing.

For instance, a person at the music festival might focus on a very specific point relating to what's on the stage. That person can move the focus outward to concentrate on a variety of features. The things that are included in the zoom-lens model can be as large or specific as one might want it to be. It takes longer for someone to process data when the lens is zoomed outward or inward. For instance, a person might take a few extra minutes to look at everything when the lens is broad and includes many stimuli. But when the focus is on a certain thing, it becomes easier to process something.

How Selective Attention Impacts Fears and Moods

How does attention relate to fears and other mental concerns? A person might place a spotlight on a specific worry or problem they have. A person who has a fear of something might focus on one object that the person is afraid of. That person would have to transition to another platform of thought when trying to manage their emotions and thoughts. The zoom-lens motion may be used to focus on the item that scares someone and causes that person to have an intense fear or a sense of anxiety. This might include a review of everything that surrounds the triggering item, thus causing a person to want to avoid situations that might include that item.

The spotlight function would cause a person to concentrate on the individual item and nothing else. This might include an unhealthy fixation on a singular stimulus. This could be a sign of an intense fear. The goal of managing these two points is to get clues as to what someone might be worried about. It is naturally preferable for the spotlight function to work to identify the root cause, but the zoom-lens concept may work just as well.

Divided Attention and Multi-Tasking

Sometimes a person can keep attention on many things. This refers to divided attention. It is where people might be concentrated on several things at the same time. Let's go back to Michael and his dinner. Michael could have the divided attention of many things in his space. He might have his attention toward both the people he is eating with at the dinner table and the surroundings in the area. He might place his divided attention on all the people who are also dining. Michael could also place a focus on other people who are in a space or the ambiance of the restaurant.

The divided attention that Michael uses will help him get more out of his dining experience. He will both enjoy his time and pay attention to the people he is dining with. At the same time, his attention is not going to be laser-focused. He will think about the entire picture and bring it all together to create a memory or vision that is distinct and unique in some fashion.

People who have fears can place their divided attention of many things to get over their fears. They might look at not only the object one is afraid of but also the context that the object is in, the surroundings, the feelings of people surrounding something, and so forth. Having a divided attention helps to look at many things at the same time. Divided attention should be used responsibly for the best results. Although it helps to look at many things at once, doing so could also be dangerous if a person does not concentrate enough on their surroundings. What does multi-tasking have to do with this point? Multi-tasking helps people be able to understand when several tasks have to be done. The goal is to see what tasks have come about and how those tasks can be resolved quickly.

People who multitask will place their divided attention on everything they can do. A person in an office might think about all the jobs that have to be done in a single day and gradually work on them. Someone in a school might also look at all the finals or exams one has and spend time throughout the day studying each one at varying times. Sometimes multi-tasking can destroy or hamper one's concentration. A person might forget about one task and will mess up on another due to a lapse in memory. Forgetting about something might hurt that person's ability to move forward with a task at hand. Even worse, the tasks that have to be completed might not be handled as well as one might have wished.

Dual-task interference might take place. In this situation, two cognitive tasks are being handled at once. This makes it harder for a person to concentrate on what one might want to do. A person might think about something positive, but a negative stimulus might be crowding that person's mind. Those two may interact with each other to create a sense of fear in one's mind. This can be very dangerous.

Continuous partial attention may also occur in some cases. In this situation, the focus one has is consistently split between many tasks. The person is not paying full attention to everything one is doing. This lack of attention makes it harder for a person to think about what one might be doing when trying to do two things at once. These concerns are important to explore with regards to trying to manage one's attention on many things. Although a person might have several root issues relating to anxiety or other issues, there often comes a time where those worries have to be controlled carefully to keep a problem from being worse. The cautious move would be to avoid handling too many things at once. Overwhelming one's mind with issues surrounding multiple problems would make it harder for someone to think clearly.

It might be best to resolve mental issues by focusing on one point at a time. A single root cause might be considered when trying to manage depression or anger. Knowing how to target that one thing is vital for ensuring the problems in one's life are considered the right way. Having a sensible idea of what to expect to manage fears or other worries is essential.

Chapter 9 – Identifying How Someone Pays Attention

Attention is not as easy to measure. While anyone might assume that attention works by looking at how much time it takes for a person to respond to a certain concern or question and how effectively that person can respond. This also includes knowing how someone might respond in a positive or negative way. In the cognitive psychology world, a person might start paying attention more to something negative in nature. That negativity comes as a person becomes too afraid of what one might be seeing. That person will become scared of something and frustrated over that stimulus. A person who is afraid of something might respond negatively faster than when they encounter something that is positive.

To make any CBT process work, it is critical to see what people are likely to pay attention to and focus on. Several strategies can be used to review how well a person can pay attention to. These strategies may be used when testing a person to see how well they respond to stimuli. This can work in the exploration stage of a test and will move into the awareness stage to help a person notice what problems someone might have.

The Dot-Probe Test

The Dot-Probe test helps to determine what is causing a person to feel nervous or worried about something.

The steps for using the Dot-Probe test are as follows:

1. Produce two separate stimuli. The first should be a neutral stimulus while the second is a threatening one.

The stimuli that are to be used will vary based on the issues. For instance, Dan has a fear of dogs and needs help with resolving the issue. He might be subjected to multiple stimuli. The first can be a field with no dogs in it while the second may be the same field, but this time a dog or two.

2. The first of the stimuli would be displayed on the screen - the image of the field without dogs.

3. The second stimulus, which is the one that could be deemed as being threatening to Dan, should be projected next - the image of the field with the dog.

The goal is to notice how quickly Dan notices the dog. By observing how he responds to the Dot-Probe test, it becomes easier to confirm that Dan has a problem with the dog.

The Emotional Stroop Test

Another test for gauging one's attention is the Emotional Stroop Test. In this test, a few steps are used to figure out which words or ideas might be identified by a person as being overly threatening.

1. Display a series of neutral words.

The words should be ones that do not relate to the fear or worry that someone has. In Dan's case, the words might be ones that relate heavily to everyday things.

2. A series of threatening words should be displayed next.

Words relating to dogs would be displayed toward Dan in this case. Dan will see words that link up to what he is afraid of.

3. Measure how long it takes for the person to identify the certain words that came about in the exam.

The amount of time needed for a person to respond verbally should be examined. Dan should have less time identifying the non-threatening words than what he would spend reviewing the ones that are frightening or cause him anxiety. The test will reveal that someone is struggling with some issues surrounding a dramatic problem.

The Visual Search Test

What bothers someone is easier to identify than other stimuli. In Dan's case, he would notice the dog in a large setting. He might focus on that dog more than anything else because he sees the dog as threatening and harmful. The visual search test is asking a person to view a space to see what might be present. The search process can be extensive and often challenging. Those who identify certain items in a field or other space first might express fears or have certain attitudes that predispose them toward particular feelings.

Why It's Important to Test Attention

The most interesting part of attention is that it often influences how well a person is able to recognize something. The brain will respond to certain things faster than to other things. By identifying what that person is responding to the fastest, it is easier to determine what problems might be persistent in one's life and what has to be resolved or explored. Knowing how to test one's attention is critical in treating one's internal issues. Having a good plan for managing fear and keeping the issue in question from being a threat is helpful to ease fears. The reviews of a test for one's attention can be vital for looking at what causes a person to experience certain feelings.

Chapter 10 – Resolving Issues Relating to Attention Through CBT

CBT helps people recognize what they can do to keep their issues relating to CBT from being a burden. This chapter concentrates on the use of cognitive behavioral therapy to help a person to focus one's attention on things. Anxieties and other worries do not have to be a burden if the right moves are used to fix a problem.

1. Take note of the regular distractions one might have.

This first step is to look at how distractions might influence one's ability to maintain attention. CBT suggests that many people fail to pay attention to things because they like to focus more on everyday items that they are familiar with. It is through these distractions that it becomes easier for people to feel encouraged or motivated to do something. The distractions can be frustrating at times and often a challenge. These include issues like checking one's phone, rummaging through one's wallet to see that it is organized, looking at television monitors, watching the clock and so forth. A plan must be made to keep those distractions under control before they get worse. Try to write down at least twenty distractions that might occur in a day.

2. Be more perceptive of what is in an area.

Perception might be different from attention and should make it easier for people to feel confident and comfortable with whatever they wish to accomplish.

3. Be willing to ask more questions.

The best way for people to pay attention is to be ready to ask questions. Those who ask more questions will feel positive about how they are managing their lives and will understand more about what they want to do.

4. Keep notes on what one notices by hand.

A good idea for keeping notes is to take a look at what someone can do to be comfortable. Notes can be taken by hand with a small pad or with a phone or other device. This requires an extra bit of effort, but it helps people to recall information. It is easier to remember things and to take notes when the content is manually jotted down.

5. Observe how people respond to certain stimuli or how the things one notices might influence what they do.

Paying attention helps people to notice what others are doing and why they feel certain ways. This might help people to see how certain processes work as well. Knowing how those things come about helps people to clear up misconceptions or worries about certain items or issues they might potentially encounter.

6. After a period of time, check back on the list of distractions and see how many were found.

Note all of the distractions that took place and see how often they were pervasive or otherwise prevalent in one's line of thinking, how often they occurred or how long a person was bothered by them.

7. Keep working on this practice a few times in a week. Take note of how well one is able to pay attention versus the distractions that one encountered.

By improving upon one's attention, the perception someone holds will improve.

Take the Long Road

To build attention, a person has to spend some extra time looking at things. This includes reading books or reports all the way through and not just the summaries but also observing physical items and seeing as many details as one can find. The goal is to build upon one's perception and ability to notice things. At the start, a person might feel bored with all the attention that has to be placed on certain things. With practice, a person will have better attention and focus. The mind will be used to looking at certain stimuli or ideas for an extended period of time. The growth in one's mind for handling more information is a necessity to increase one's ability to manage more complicated ideas and concepts.

Can This Work for Those With ADHD?

In addition to managing one's attention through CBT, the practice may also work for those who have attention deficit or hyperactivity disorder or ADHD. Originally thought to be an issue in children, ADHD can occur at any time in one's life. ADHD is not always easy to manage as the brain is not able to perform many tasks or functions at once. However, those who have ADHD would require extra observation to ensure that the CBT process works well enough. People with this disorder often struggle to keep their attention on things, thus making it harder to manage one's focus. Several attempts at using CBT might be required in this instance.

Chapter 11 – The Most Common Cognitive Distortions

Cognitive behavioral therapy can focus on reviewing cognitive distortions. These are issues where a person's mental processes are not organized as well as they should be. It is through these distortions that it becomes easy for someone to feel nervous or frustrated with things in life. The exploration process of cognitive therapy should focus on how well a person's mental functions are working via these distortions. The reshaping process will help to absolve these distortions before they can become worse.

The Basics of a Distortion

Cognitive distortions are formed when a person starts to think about something that might not be correct or appropriate. In many cases, such distortions will form because a person is too busy thinking about certain things and creating generalizations. A distortion can develop out of fear or from some pessimistic attitude. For instance, one man might assume that the woman he is dating is upset because he did something wrong. This leads him into a spiral of negative thinking. The distortion would lead him into thinking the wrong ideas as the woman might have been upset over something else entirely. She may have been upset about something that had nothing to do with him and he is worrying unnecessarily. Cognitive distortions are often destructive and difficult for people to live with.

Filtering

Filtering occurs when a person ignores many of the things that come about in one's life and focuses more on the negative thoughts. This happens when a person might be overly self-judgmental. To understand this, let's look at Harry and his concerns surrounding dating. He might be afraid of dating because he is fearful of what women might think about him. As he works on his thoughts, he finds it hard for him to recognize all the good things about himself.

Harry might have plenty of positive things happen to him while at a speed dating event. He might have found several women who like certain things about him. At the same time, there might have been one or two women out of ten that he did not impress. He might have introduced himself the wrong way or might have become nervous around those women. Harry would filter out his experiences and concentrate less on the successes he had with most of the women and just focus on that one person that he thought he failed to impress. He will feel upset and fearful because he knows that he did something wrong and was not confident about it.

Black and White Thinking

Black and white thinking is a distortion that could also be called an all-or-nothing approach. Either a person is successful with something or that person is a failure.

In Harry's case, he would think about his efforts in dating in two ways:

1. White – Harry is happy with his date because everything went well. He did not make a fool of himself, nor did he embarrass the woman he was dating.

2. Black – Harry feels that the date was a total failure because he made one mistake on the date. He might have done exceptionally well with everything else, but it was a single mistake that he made that he feels his girlfriend is going to remember.

Harry does not understand that the woman he was with is going to see him beyond the issues he thinks he had. He will be focused on the worries about that one mistake and it may not have been a mistake at all.

Magnification or Minimization

This two-pronged cognitive distortion is a problem that can negatively influence a person:

1. Magnification – A problem becomes much worse to one's mind than what it really is.

2. Minimization – A problem is not treated as important as it should be.

A good example might be what can happen when a car needs an oil change. A person might magnify the problem and feel that the engine in the car could break down any time soon, thus keeping that person from wanting to use that car even when that person has an absolute need for it. Minimization is when a person thinks that an oil change is not all that big of a deal. This could lead to engine damage. The person might not notice this just now, but the threat could be dramatic.

For Harry's scenario involving dating, he might magnify a single problem like his hair not being combed properly. He might feel that this is a huge deal-breaker for a date, but this problem might not be important at all. He magnifies the issue and thinks too much about it when there is no need for doing so in the first place. If Harry was to use the opposite approach and thought less about something, he would be minimizing the issue in question. He would be underestimating the concern. Either extreme is risky as it makes it harder for a person to feel positive.

Overgeneralization

An overgeneralization is a problem where someone might be thinking too much about one thing. For example, Harry might over generalize his girlfriend's negative response to something she saw at the restaurant they were visiting. She might have responded to some other person's outfit, thinking that it was not appropriate for the season. Harry could have thought differently. He might over generalize and assume that she was upset with something he was doing. The biggest problem with overgeneralizations is that people often experience these even when there is no reason to do so. It is often difficult for people to ask questions of others about how they feel. Sometimes it might be inappropriate to ask those questions, or someone might at least struggle to ask questions.

Jumping to Conclusions

The act of jumping to conclusions is similar to overgeneralization in that this practice involves someone assuming that an event will go in one way without thinking that conclusion they are making is sensible or realistic. A person who jumps to conclusions will assume that one statement or action will mean the same thing to everyone each time that is experienced. When Harry hears from his date that she is uncomfortable, he might jump to the conclusion that his demeanor is making her feel that way. This could cause him to panic and worry. The truth could be that she is just cold because the air conditioning is on too high, but Harry would assume the worst and think he's doing something wrong. Jumping to conclusions entails a person not thinking about a scenario. The big picture is not being seen.

Personalization

Personalization occurs when someone thinks that everything that happens is all about them and that person's actions. Harry might notice that the people at the restaurant appear to be rushed. He would personalize the situation and assume that his general appearance has caused the situation at the restaurant to become intense. All the people at that restaurant might seem rushed or stressed, but what Harry doesn't know is that the place is short-staffed and not about him personally. The most important part of personalization is that this comes from the person's mind being overly self-centered while focusing on only one part of the experience. The lack of attention might keep that someone from focusing and understanding what is really going on.

A Desire to Be Right

There are often times when a person demands to be right all the time and will refuse to accept what is really happening. That person might be more concerned with being right all the time. This might occur even in cases where someone is trying to look one's best. In Harry's situation, he might be trying to show he is right by concentrating on how well the evening is going and what he is doing. He is trying to see that all the moves he is making during his date are going along right. Harry might think that he is doing the right thing, but he will become down on himself when he notices that his date is not happy. He could become overly upset with himself when he notices that what he is doing is not working as well as he might have wished.

Having a desire to be right is also about trying to make that person look great in public. People who are seen as always wanting to be right might be treated better by the public, or at least that is what people who follow this cognitive distortion might feel. Harry might assume that he needs to be right all the time for his date to recognize him as a trustworthy person worth dating. What Harry does not understand is that his date is not necessarily expecting him to be right all the time. She knows that not everyone is perfect, and she is willing to accept Harry for who he is. The distortion that Harry experiences makes it harder for him to accept this. Instead of trying to keep a sense of mental control, Harry has started to focus more on the negative things that have come about in his mind because of being wrong in some fashion.

The Fallacy of Change

It is impossible for people to change every single thing around them. People might assume that they can do anything and bend the world to their will if they just think about what they are doing to control others. This leads to the issue known as the fallacy of change. The fallacy of change entails the following issues:

1. A person engages in a certain action.

2. That someone assumes other people or things in a situation will change based on what they did.

3. The person will wait to see what happens. When nothing happens, that initial person will feel upset or ashamed.

Let's go back to Harry's situation. He might bring his date in a ride-sharing vehicle to get to a certain location for the event. Harry would expect the ride-sharing driver to respect the two of them and to be cautious and careful while on the road. At the same time, the driver might not pay attention to how he is driving and instead engage in the same behaviors one is used to having while driving alone. Harry might think that the driver will change his attitude while driving, but that is not going to happen. Harry is experiencing the fallacy of change. He is unsuccessful at trying to change someone else's behavior because he is too busy struggling to think about what he can do to make the driver change his behavior.

Heaven's Reward Fallacy

The heaven's reward fallacy is when a person believes that any good act will be repaid in some fashion. The person in this situation will feel that he or she deserves something for everything they do. This fallacy is based on the idea that he or she has received the things they have wanted often in the past. A person who is overly spoiled will have noticed that he or she received many things in life even when they did not necessarily deserve them. This creates the false belief that everything will go someone's way and that there's no need to fear about a wish not coming true.

Harry would do many things in his date to make it go right. He might give his date his coat to keep her warm, but he may use the heaven's reward fallacy to assume that what he is doing will be rewarded. He would expect her to do something in return. As the evening progresses, he realizes that he is giving much and is not getting anything in return. The fallacy makes him feel as though he has done nothing to have his date feel good about the evening. This, in turn, creates a dramatic fallacy where he is not happy about what he is doing.

By resolving this issue through CBT, Harry might recognize that demanding everything from the world would be a selfish and ungenerous thing to do. It is through CBT that it becomes easier for someone's mind to be grounded by acknowledging the errors in thinking. Each of the cognitive distortions must be targeted in cognitive behavioral therapy. The analysis process must look into what is causing a person to feel such issues so they can be targeted accordingly.

Resolving Distortions

The main goal of managing cognitive distortions is to reverse them and to allow one's mind to feel stronger and more constructive. Cognitive distortions can be resolved by using a few basic steps in the CBT process:

1. Start by identifying the distortion in question.

2. Look at the realistic nature of the distortion. Is there something wrong with the thought?

3. Look at the evidence surrounding the distortion being produced.

4. Talk with others about the distortions.

5. Think about the alternatives that can be utilized by taking old ideas and replacing them with new thoughts.

6. Use a scale to evaluate things using a scale of 0 to 10. If the problem is significant and is hurting one's life, it could get a ten and if it is trivial would be measured at four or lower.

7. Establish a series of definitions for personal feelings or attitudes.

8. Look at any outside factors and try not to blame the issues on themselves.

Let's go back one last time to the situation involving Harry and his struggles to find a woman that he will enjoy being with. Harry might have struggled to stay emotionally healthy due to struggles like personalization or jumping to conclusions. He can absolve himself of these issues by using a few basic points:

- Look at what has caused him to experience such a distortion.

- Review how intense or significant some of the problems that caused the distortion might be. This includes looking at problems that might not really be problems at all.

- See what he thinks about certain problems.

- Prepare new definitions based on the problems he has come across. These include new ideas that will improve upon what he wants to think.

- He will eventually notice that it is not hard for him to manage a public situation once he sees that the issues he has have been a challenge to manage.

Cognitive distortions are problems that make it harder for people to realize what is really happening. It is through these distortions that a person might become overly frustrated or angry about a situation. Resolving such distortions is the best thing that someone can do to be successful.

Chapter 12 – Fact vs. Opinion – How to Manage Both

Understanding how cognitive distortions work can make a difference in managing the problems that one might experience. However, there is an even more important concern and that is managing the difference between facts and opinions. This is a basic aspect of managing one's mind. While many people understand the facts, some people have fallen into the belief that what they are seeing is the truth even if it is not backed up by facts. One of the greatest reasons why people experience fear and other problems is because they don't understand the difference between opinions and facts. There is a test that may be used to help understand the difference between facts and opinions.

What Causes a Person to Misconstrue Facts and Opinions?

The main reason people mix up their details is due to how they might suffer from one of many cognitive distortions. Those distortions can be intense and pervasive enough so that one's memories might become fabricated or distorted. Whether it is the validity effect making things real or imagination inflation impacting one's general perception, the threats that can come out of such a situation as this must be understood. The false misconceptions can happen from experience, but in some cases, they might come from someone being fatigued or unaware of what is happening. A lack of awareness and consideration can make it harder for someone to manage the things one wishes to do. It is frustrating, but these issues of misinterpreting can happen and might be a challenge.

The Basic Test

It is time to look at the test to determine how well someone can compare factors and opinions. The steps involved are as follows:

1. Find a worksheet that includes a series of statements about one's life.

It is easy to find worksheets online. These worksheets should include a series of simple statements relating to one's life. Such statements may include the following:

- I am a good person.
- Someone yelled at me for some reason.
- I am hard to get along with.
- My next project is going to be a mess.
- I am not ready to do things to assist others.
- I did not help a friend of mine when I was supposed to.

These statements can vary, so investigate online to see what is available to find a fact vs. opinion worksheet.

2. Answer the questions on the worksheet. These should be answered as a fact or opinion.

The important thing is that there is always going to be a right or wrong answer to each question. Saying "I am hard to get along with" or "My next project is going to be a mess" is essentially some kind of opinion.

Saying "I did not help a friend of mine…" could be seen as a fact.

The questions should be seen as hypotheticals. The test-taker should look at the statements and see how they could be realistically answered.

> 3. Review the answers that were given versus the correct answers that were supposed to be given.

At this point, the person will notice what types of thoughts one has and will recognize how emotionally charged someone's attitudes might be. By identifying the wrong answers one gives, it becomes easier to identify the problems that someone has. This includes working to handle some of the ongoing mental or emotional concerns that one has developed. Having a smart plan for identifying the problems one has based on the answers helps to give someone an idea of what issues need to be resolved. Further CBT strategies can be used to fix these problems.

The Main Goal

It is not uncommon for people to experience certain problems relating to what they think are opinions versus what are facts. People who fear the worst might develop those fears due to some of the misconceptions that one has. With a fact vs. opinion test, a person will start to realize that some of these problems are unrealistic and need to be resolved.

Chapter 13 – The Learning Experience

Learning is a lifelong activity that happens well beyond childhood. While it is true that the adult brain might not take in new things as quickly as children can, it is essential for adults to keep learning things and to investigate new ideas. Learning is a part of CBT that concentrates on how well a person is capable of getting over fear and learning how to live a more positive and productive life. Through learning, a person will develop strong and productive associations. By working hard, a person can learn how to recover from a fear or other emotional concern.

How Are Ideas Introduced?

It is through the unique content and concepts in the learning process that a task can be more effective and easier to do. People who work hard to learn new ideas will have an easier time managing their lives and making their knowledge more intriguing.

The ideas that come about when learning can include:

- A person will see something new that is very different from what one might have seen elsewhere.

- The new stimulus being presented will be compared with other things that someone has explored and reviewed in the past.

- The new meaning of the stimulus is then paired into a proper area of one's memory based on how it relates to other ideas one has studied before.

The process for introducing new items will take some time depending on one's ability to adapt to the new content being introduced. In some cases, a person might be ready to take in new data in just a matter of minutes. In other instances, it will take repetition and reinforcement for that person to retain a new idea. The goal is to allow the new idea to be linked in the brain so it can be recalled easily later. Anything that enters into the user's long-term memory in lieu of the working memory is always a plus. Why is this critical in CBT? It is through learning that a person can find a way to replace negative thoughts with something that can be associated with other ideas one has learned. The new stimulus does not have to be any stronger than the old one. It just has to be persistent and unique enough so that the new idea can be recalled and used effectively.

Actions Become Automatic

Those that complete actions more often will have an easier time recalling them and retaining them in their memories. This is especially the case with procedural learning as people learn how to do things based on the repeated actions and processes they go through. This is vital for CBT as it shows that for a person to change their behaviors or thought processes, actions have to be regularly reinforced. A person cannot just change one's mind or actions by learning about something just once. They have to be trained long enough with enough reinforcements to keep from forgetting the new idea. Instead of having to force negative ideas out of one's mind, they will quickly be displaced by the repeated actions involved in the new idea and the person will evolve emotionally.

How Long Can Memories Last?

The long-term memory one develops will last much longer than the working memory that only runs for a few hours or days at a time.

There are many rules regarding how long memories might last after they are learned:

- The everyday use of something is critical. The new things being learned might stick in one's brain for a while if the content is something that can work in one's everyday life and through daily procedures.

- Anything involving procedures might last for a longer period of time provided that such procedures are repeated.

- The general efforts surrounding one's studies could be a factor. Those who study more often and work a little harder to learn certain concepts will be more likely to succeed and thrive in their studies.

Every person will respond to certain memories and learning processes differently.

A Note About Learning

The learning experience is something that makes life worth exploring. Anyone can learn new things at any point in one's life. However, it is often easier for people who are younger to learn more. As the brain develops, it becomes easy for people to learn new concepts. Children do well with learning new things because their brains are still developing and evolving. As their brains change over time, it becomes easier for them to think more about what they are doing with their thoughts and actions. Those who can do well with those mental functions will be more likely to succeed and thrive in their lives.

A growing brain may become larger when it learns new things. When a child learns a new skill, a series of new synapses are formed within the brain. Such synapses link to new functions, thus allowing someone to plan new ideas and movements. Having extra control over one's mind at this juncture can help anyone to grow as the brain becomes a little stronger. Although children learn new things quickly, that does not mean an adult cannot learn easily. It is through learning that it becomes easier for people to have healthier and stronger lives.

Chapter 14 – Triggers and Causes

Triggers and causes are two things that can influence how depression and other problems in life might develop. While the terms triggers and causes might be similar to each other, they are each very different.

The best way to explain triggers and causes is to look at a very simple comparison:

1. A cause is something that involves a certain feeling to happen.
2. A trigger is a stimulus that will make the cause more intense.

Triggers and causes can directly influence many worries that someone might have or struggle with.

Triggers

A person might experience a trigger after going through one of the many causes of a person developing anxiety or a fear. There are a few specific examples of triggers that can be named. For instance, a person might become anxious about not having a clean house. There might be certain triggers that can occur to make the anxiety worse. These could be spotting some dust or a stained sink. This trigger will make the anxiety worse because that person will worry that the house is becoming increasingly dirty. This could lead to cleaning the house excessively.

Another example might be from how the lawn outside one's house might grow to an excessive height. That person might not be keen on mowing a lawn, but the added length of the lawn could trigger an anxiety about caring for the lawn. A trigger will make a bad situation worse than it has to be. Those who notice these triggers might see that there could be another issue that causes a person to become afraid and nervous of what might happen. Remember, the trigger is the link to the cause. Knowing the trigger is vital to discovering a cause that might take place and make a situation worse.

Can Added Time to Think Make Triggers More Severe?

Many people like to relax and have fun in their lives. They like to have certain distractions and feel relaxed. A trigger might cause a person to be overly afraid of a situation that might occur because they have had too much time to think. A person who has too much time to think about things will start to have unrealistic thoughts. This includes cases where someone might think about the negative things in life and what could happen if certain problems occur. When these thoughts evolve and erupt, it becomes a challenge for people to move forward and make their lives peaceful.

The main reason why people think extra time to think can make worries and problems harder is that the human imagination can roam rather quickly. It only takes a few moments for a person to start thinking about the many scenarios that can come along in a situation. The fears and worries one develops can be worse and hard for many to manage if not run right. A person should try to create a limit as to how long a person might think about a trigger for. Knowing how to keep the trigger that one has from being too intense or hard should be examined accordingly. The worries that one has could be dramatic if not handled accordingly.

How Can a Trigger Be Identified?

The greatest problem about triggers is that it is often difficult for people to identify them. Sometimes a trigger will automatically occur without that person thinking about what is happening. When the trigger is identified, it becomes easier for the issue at hand to be resolved.

There are a few things that can be done to identify a trigger:

1. Look at the cause of one's fear or other negative emotion.

2. Notice when that negative emotion is produced.

3. Review the scenario in which the changes took place. What events took place? Were there certain problems that made the situation at hand worse than it needed to be?

4. Look at the specific changes in emotions that might have happened. These include cases where someone becomes worried, afraid, or more angry than usual. Knowing the specific change will help identify the trigger.

5. Determine where or what was happening during the triggering event. Sometimes this might require observing a change a few times to determine what precisely caused the trigger.

Can Multiple Triggers Occur At the Same Time?

The human brain is complicated and several triggers might occur at a time. These multiple triggers can prove to be a burden to one's mind, but they will directly influence what someone might be thinking or feeling. Sometimes an irrational thought or fear will come about due to two or more triggers occurring at the same time. One trigger might be a little stronger than others.

For instance, a person who is afraid of dogs might be triggered by not only the ringing of a bell on a dog's collar but also from its barking and growling. However, the fear might not be so intense when just the ringing of the bell takes place. When the dog's growling starts to become pervasive it becomes clear that the dog would be an even bigger threat. The fear will only become worse due to the ongoing worry that the dog could bite or chase them.

How to Decide Which Triggers Are the Most Intense

The main goal of handling triggers is to look at which ones might be the strongest. Having a clear idea of which triggers are stronger than others helps people to understand what problems might have to be corrected the soonest. These steps may be used:

1. Take note of all the cases when someone's fear was triggered.

2. Look at the stimuli that were present. Review the sights, sounds, and other sensory details that led to the fear occurring.

3. Notice how intense the fear was based on those stimuli. Try to rate the situation from 0 to 10 if possible.

4. Keep an ongoing list of occasions when a fear is triggered to identify what the main triggers might be.

5. Be willing to include new triggers as they happen.

Sometimes a person will notice that the triggers are hardly anything to be afraid of. In other instances, the triggers might be more burdensome or worrying that only make one's mentally disturbed. This practice might take a few weeks to complete, but spending a bit of time gives anyone a closer look at the situation or issue that is causing a fear to develop and how that problem can be corrected or eliminated.

Causes

Many causes that someone might experience can be hard to live with due to the fears one might experience in life. Fears, depression, and other problems are caused by many events. They might happen due to personal experiences or observations. They might occur due to certain situations that someone has experienced. The cause will lead to many triggers. To understand this, it helps to look at a certain example. Let's say that Kim is worried about her health. She might be afraid of having a heart attack. The cause of her fear could be because her family has a history of heart attacks. Perhaps someone in her family had a heart attack recently. This history will make Kim fear that she will have a heart attack herself.

What would cause her fear to be triggered? That fear of a heart attack is not going to appear all the time, but some trigger will bring that fear to the surface. Kim might hear a story on the television about heart attacks and how they are being managed in hospitals. She might also see a television commercial promoting some medication that promises to help prevent people who have had such attacks from having second ones. The stories and things that Kim sees will cause her to think about heart attacks and her risk of having one. This would cause her to possibly take in some unreasonable measures.

Kim's triggers are based on the same cause of her fear or anxiety. Those triggers become a burden to handle, but it is through understanding what causes them to link to the roots of a fear or other worry that makes the treatment process effective. Kim would have an easier time handling the situation at hand if she learned more about the positive things that she could do.

The Value of Healing

The worries that people might have can be dramatic and significant. It is through cognitive psychology that the triggers and causes of fears and anxieties can be resolved and managed before they get worse. Understanding the causes and triggers is important because it helps anyone to resolve certain problems or worries one might have one life. It does not take much time for a person to heal when the problems are identified and the correct actions are used to keep those issues from being a burden. The main goal is to create a sense of support and comfort in dealing with those issues.

Learning about triggers and causes can help anyone to be honest with themselves. It is through this honesty that it becomes easier for a person to resolve mental problems that one has. Knowing how to get these issues in check and to keep from being any worse is a necessity for resolving the fears one holds.

Chapter 15 – Understanding Fear

Now it is time to look at how well individual problems in one's life can be targeted through CBT and cognitive psychology. CBT is designed to help alleviate the problems people have based on their thought processes and how they pay attention. To start, it helps to look at fear, one of the most basic emotions. The next few chapters in this guide focus on fear, a concept that often paralyzes people and keeps them from living the lives that they want to lead.

A Basic Consideration of Fear

Fear is a natural part of life. It is through fear that people make decisions over what they want to avoid and what they are comfortable with. Fears can be about anything. Some people even like to claim that they fear nothing, but deep down there is always some emotion that may be felt that triggers worries or fears in someone's mind. It is through fear that people become afraid and worried about the things that they come across and get themselves involved in. Everyone has fears in their lives. Sometimes those fears can become more of a burden than they have to be. Such worries and concerns in one's life can grow and blossom to be dramatic issues that can hamper one's ability to function. The good news is that fears can be controlled.

Fear occurs when a person feels that something is dangerous or is likely to cause harm in some fashion. The threat of certain stimuli might be too much for a person, thus causing them to be afraid. The threat can cause the status quo in one's mind to be dramatically shifted. As the fear is ignited, that person starts to feel a sense of panic. This makes it harder for a person to properly function because their mind will be filled with the worries that come from the fears that a person has. It is through those fears that someone might make some difficult decisions including irrational moves designed just to avoid the fears that one has.

What Causes Fears to Develop

Every person develops new fears at multiple stages in their lives. The most common way how someone might develop a fear is through some traumatic experience a person had. This is especially the case with one's childhood as it might be tough to live with. Everyone develops fears at some point in life, but the points that will contribute to the fears someone has can be extensive. These are some of the most difficult worries that someone might come across when there are certain problems:

- People who get into difficult or negative events in the past might be likely to develop fears. This is especially for those who are younger. It is easier for children to develop fears.

- Fears also occur when a person does not have control over a situation. It is easier for people to feel confident and fearless when they know what they can do and that they are in charge of the situations they encounter.

- People who are taught to fear things might develop fears. Sometimes this might come from the validity effect where false ideas are treated as reality.

- Generalizations are common in fears. A person might assume that all cats or dogs are dangerous or that all airplanes are likely to break apart and kill people, for instance.

- Cognitive distortions may also be a threat. A person who thinks the wrong ideas or makes the wrong assumptions can develop irrational fears.

These fears can form at various times in someone's life, but the specific nature of the fear and the reasoning for it may be different based on age and how rational they are when thinking about their fears.

Association With Certain Things

An important part of fears is that they are often caused by the associations people have toward certain things. They might link certain stimuli to something else. For instance, a child might be afraid of the dark after hearing a door slam at night. The child might become afraid because the dark represents the unpleasant sound of a door slamming. The sudden exposure that a person has to negative things can be dramatic and difficult to manage. The worries someone has could be even worse when that person experiences a highly traumatic event. The concept of fears developing by association is a point that was analyzed by John B. Watson in the early twentieth century. In his experiment, he used a procedure that would show how specific events can cause people to become afraid:

1. Watson exposed a young boy to a rat among other furry creatures. The boy did not have any fears or adverse feelings toward any of the animals.

2. Watson then produced a difficult sound that would be paired with the exposure to the animal. For instance, he would produce a sound like a hammer banging loudly on a wooden plank. This sound would be produced when the animal appears.

3. The child would become fearful of the sound. Eventually, that child would link that sound with the exposure to animals.

The psychological experiment that Watson produced shows that when something is paired with a negative experience, it becomes easier for someone to develop a fear.

The Amygdala

There is a certain part of the brain that dictates how fears are developed within one's mind. This section of the brain is the amygdala. Found deep within the temporal lobe, the amygdala is a very small part of the brain, but its value is how it produces fears and other sensations in the body. The amygdala identifies emotions including feelings sparked by stimuli that might be threatening to one's life. This part of the brain takes in many of the sensory details. It is through the amygdala that decisions are made about what one needs to do. Any disruptions that might take place within the brain can be dangerous and potentially harmful. Further research is needed to fully understand how the amygdala links to others parts of the brain. After all, the brain is the most complicated organ in the human body.

The Hippocampus

Although the amygdala is the most important part of the brain with regards to fears and other disturbing emotions, the hippocampus cannot be ignored. Located under the cerebral cortex, this is the part of the brain that stores memories and feelings. As a fearful or stressful situation evolves, the hippocampus will pick up the memories associated with it. The memories could be positive or negative. When the situation is negative, the amygdala will identify what is happening in the hippocampus, thus triggering the difficult response in one's body.

The Prefrontal Cortex

The prefrontal cortex is located in the front lobe and is part of the human brain that is the most frontal. This section of the brain is responsible for the decision-making. The prefrontal cortex is very important based on how well it functions and retrieves thoughts. This section will be stressed by the amygdala that triggers the physical responses that accompany fear. This keeps that part of the brain from acting rationally. This could cause a person to make an illogical decision that might be dangerous or harmful.

The prefrontal cortex and hippocampus are different from the amygdala, but it is clear that the stresses in the body that the amygdala produces will be a challenge to handle at times. Knowing how to control one's fears is critical as it keeps the amygdala from being negatively impacted and will not produce more stresses than what one can handle.

Fears Developed in Youth

Fears that develop at a young age can persist for years. This is because the brain is still forming at the time a fear develops. As the negative feelings toward something develop in a child's brain, that child becomes fearful.

For instance, a 30-year-old woman would not be likely to develop a fear of dogs if a dog bounded up to her with a wagging tail. She would know that the dog is being friendly and that it isn't going to hurt her. That woman is unlikely to suffer from a fear of dogs. She has the rational understanding of knowing that the dog, in this case, is happy and comfortable to be around. If she experienced this situation while she was three or four years old, things would be different. Her brain at the time would still be forming. It would be difficult for her to make rational decisions or judgments about encountering a dog. She might assume that a dog running along and playing around her might be trying to hurt her.

As a result of that second instance, she would develop a fear of dogs because she worried about what they would do when she was a child. She might think that dogs are going to hurt her and that they are dangerous. There are several specific stages in which a person may develop a fear. These stages focus mainly on different types of things that a person might encounter:

1. **Infancy.** Startling feelings may come about at a very early age. A toddler or infant might experience being startled by various stimuli that one is exposed to at such an age. These effects happen as the child is only getting used to some of the things they encounter in everyday life.

2. **Six months of age.** Children start to show fears of more concrete things when they reach six months in age. A child might be afraid of strangers. That child might also be afraid of being separated from the parents.

3. **1-2 years.** Children will start to recognize that they do not have full control over everything in their lives. This, in turn, makes it easier for children to become afraid of things that they have not encountered before. It is not surprising that children would develop fears of vehicles, animals, or other things that they cannot control at this age.

4. **3-5 years.** A child's imagination starts to blossom at this point. It is here that a child will start to feel afraid and worried about many things that he or she cannot directly control or manage. Children might become afraid of the dark and anything else that feels scary. Sometimes imaginary fears may develop; the classic fear of monsters under the bed is common at this point.

5. **5-8 years.** At this age, a child's fears start to become more concrete. Children might be afraid of losing track of their parents or of getting lost. They might be afraid of various situations where they could become physically hurt. The fears at this juncture are more concrete in nature.

6. **9 years and older.** A child's fears will become more focused on things that take place outside of the home. These include fears of things that might happen in various social situations. The issues are very specific and often vivid in nature.

Adult Fears

Just because most fears develop in children does not mean they cannot develop in adults as well. It is true that adults are not as likely to experience new fears, but at the same time they might be likely to experience fears due to changing circumstances:

- An elderly person might notice many friends and family members in one's life dying. This could cause that person to develop a fear of living and dying alone.

- A lack of physical balance and strength will often result in a fear of injury or harm. This could also include a fear of heights or of situations where the body might be at risk of injury.

- As the human body changes, it becomes harder for people to develop healthy lifestyles. Individual fears relating to certain parts of the body may develop. These include fears where a person's digestive system will not stay healthy or one's joints might wear out and become painful.

The adult body produces less adrenaline. This compound produced in the brain allows a person to feel ready for anything that happens. A person who produces enough adrenaline will not be likely to fear many things. As one ages, there is less adrenaline produced, thus causing someone to start to fear more things. A person who wasn't afraid of roller coasters when young might be afraid to ride on one of them today, for instance.

Signs That Someone Is Afraid

For cognitive psychology to work when treating a person's fears, it is vital to be aware of what someone is afraid of. It is natural for people to try and hide what they fear because they are either uncomfortable with it or they are too afraid to admit that they have certain fears. There are many things to consider when determining why someone is afraid of something. The affects on the body are produced by the autonomic nervous system as natural responses to what the body might experience when encountering something a person is not comfortable with:

- The body's heart rate starts to increase. This is due to the added stress on the body and the feeling of uncertainty.

- One's rate of breathing starts to increase while trying to adapt to the increased heart rate.

- Muscles start to shake or tremble.

- The mouth becomes dry. This is because of increased breathing.

- The body also starts to perspire.

- A person might also possibly faint from all the fatigue within the body. Fainting is believed to be a defense mechanism to keep people from hurting someone.

These symptoms are produced primarily by the amygdala as it responds to the stressful situation. The response from this part of the brain is important to understand how a person is going to respond to certain things that might take place in the brain. The stress and worry that is produced at this point can be a challenge to manage, but it is through this that the brain has to respond. Not all people will show these signs of fear, but they can be quickly noticed when they do take place. The chances for a person to become afraid and worried about what might come about in one's life are strong and should be noticed carefully.

Another point to notice might be a person's hesitance to do certain things. Someone who is afraid might avoid certain situations with the belief that those concerns might be dangerous and threaten one's life. Keeping away from these situations can be a challenge for some, but they will do what they will do what they feel is vital to their survival.

Can Being Quiet Suggest Fear?

Sometimes a person will express fear without showing any visual or physical signs whatsoever. A person who is overly quiet and is not willing to say or do anything about the situation might be mentally preoccupied with the fear. As a person is motionless or quiet, they start to think too much about a problem or situation in life and what might cause it to happen. The greatest issue surrounding one's thoughts or actions is that they might be so personal that they might be uncomfortable to share them. The mind is too preoccupied with the fear when someone is silently trying to figure out the situation at hand and how to resolve the worries or other issues.

Understanding Fears

A simple search online will reveal that there are hundreds of fears that people may exhibit in their lives. There are plenty of commonplace fears like arachnophobia (fear of spiders), acrophobia (fear of heights), cynophobia (fear of dogs), and aerophobia (fear of flying). There are also some unusual fears that people hold. A person might have a fear of making decisions or decidophobia. Someone might also have gephyrophobia, a fear of bridges. Some fears are especially strange. Some people may suffer from nomophobia, a fear of going somewhere without mobile phone coverage. Others may experience somniphobia, a fear of falling asleep. There is also papaphobia, a fear of the Pope of the Catholic Church. In short, if there is something in the world, the odds are there is a fear attached to it.

What is interesting is that practically anything can be something that a person is afraid of. The conditioning for one's fears might be extensive depending on what someone might encounter or experience. It is through conditioning that a person will have an easier time with managing one's life and one's fears.

The Feararchy

There are five fears that are shared among people throughout society. Each of these fears builds upon one another into what is known as a Feararchy. Composed by Dr. Karl Albrecht, the Feararchy is a hierarchy that focuses on five fears that people may experience. These features are listed from first to fifth with the first being the base of the pyramid that the Feararchy is on and the fifth being the peak where all fears eventually end up.

1. Extinction

The most basic fear on the Feararchy pyramid is the fear of extinction. This is another way of saying that a person is afraid of death. Everyone worries about death at some point. Some people might be afraid of situations that they feel could put their lives in jeopardy. These include people who are afraid of boarding buses or airplanes or people who don't want to be in tall buildings. When a person thinks about the potential of death, they start to be afraid and worried about what might happen and the impact of one's death on other people. The fear of extinction may be threatening to people with families. A person might worry about what might happen to one's siblings, parents, spouse, or other people who are close to that person's life.

2. Mutilation

A fear of mutilation is often as intense as the fear of extinction. People are frequently afraid of what would happen if their bodies were permanently impacted by something outside of their control. The fear of mutilation is the fear of having one's body injured. This includes fears of one's body parts, organs, and other features being hurt. Sometimes people might become afraid of various animals out of the fear that those animals are going to mutilate them.

3. Loss of Autonomy

The loss of autonomy refers to the fear of being paralyzed or trapped in some way. People want to have full control over their bodies, but it becomes easy for people to lose that control from illness or from violent acts among other concerns. A loss of autonomy does not have to be strictly physical in nature. This loss may also happen when a person has no control over their relationships or social situations. That person might not be given many choices as to where to go or with whom to talk.

4. Separation

The best way to explain separation is that it is where a person is not wanted or respected by other people. In many cases, this might be a person getting the silent treatment from others. A person is rejected, abandoned, or otherwise ignored by other people. This is a highly psychological fear that focuses on how dependent a person is on someone else. When that dependence is lost or fractured, it becomes harder for a person to feel comfortable with what can happen in life. For instance, a person who has been married to someone for fifty years might be afraid of losing the person they married. The separation that occurs would make it harder for a person to feel happy about one's situation and circumstances in life.

5. Death of the Ego

The death of one's ego is a concern that cannot be ignored when looking at what causes a person to be afraid. When the ego is killed, a person will feel shame and embarrassment. This could happen when a person is wrong or judged by others in some fashion. The death of the ego is focused upon when all the other things one needs in life have been fully satisfied. It is through the ego that certain attitudes or values might develop. By working with the ego and keeping it under control, it may be easier for the human mind to be kept in check.

All of these points surrounding fears are ranked based on how commonplace they are. People are more concerned with their current safety and protection than they are of their egos, but both of these fears may occur in all people. This is similar to a fear-based version of the Maslow pyramid of needs. The fear of extinction is something that all people will go through in their lives, and it is impossible to shake due to there being so many threats in one's daily life. After a while, a person might become afraid of more things relating to one's public life and relationships toward others. Those fears come about as a person's life becomes more realized.

There is always the chance that someone might move from one part of the pyramid to another while skipping a few tiers. A person might be more concerned about the death of one's ego than that of the fear of separation. They might not have another person close to be separated from.

How Fears Can Impact Perception

It is through fear that a person's perception will quickly be impacted. When someone fears something, their perception becomes increasingly negative to the point of trying to avoid certain situations. A person who sees something or notices a thing that they are afraid of will develop added stress in the amygdala. As this area of the brain functions, it produces a sense of fear or worry in one's mind. This makes it difficult for people to feel comfortable about the situation they face that is causing fear.

The pressure within the amygdala comes from the sensory organs of the body noticing the sight, scents, sounds, and other physical characteristics of whatever someone is afraid of. The amygdala may be connected to the part of the brain that manages one's senses, although further research is needed to fully understand this concept. As the fearful stimuli are introduced, it becomes easier for a person to become afraid and worried. The stimuli will cause a person to become afraid and concerned. The worry that is produced can be damaging as it keeps that person from being capable of seeing something for what it is in reality.

When Are Fears Produced?

It is easier for people to develop fears and other strong long-term feelings when they are at a young age. Fears can develop at an early age and can become more concrete as a person ages and becomes more aware of some of the things that might cause a fear to develop.

Fears are often likely to develop at certain times:

1. They may occur from direct contact with something. This includes a contact that left a negative impact on one's mind.

2. They might develop when something bad happens to someone who is very close to another person.

3. Some fears happen from reading or hearing stories about something in a negative light.

4. They might happen by association. When a person's spouse or sibling feels a fear, that other person might start to feel the same fear.

All people respond to these fears in different ways. The struggles that can occur could be dramatic. The development of fears is important to understand when it comes to resolving them through cognitive psychology. It is also important to recall some of the memories that one has about something that might not be as pervasive but could still make an impact.

Chapter 16 – Trauma and How It Can Be Reframed

There are often times when a person might suffer from a trauma that causes them to become afraid. A trauma is something that triggers fears, causes people to become depressed, or even prompts a person to feel extensive grief for a long time. Understanding what trauma is and how it can directly influence one's life should be explored to understand what causes a person to have certain problems in life.

The Definition of a Trauma

Trauma is an event that might come out of nowhere and create a significant worry in one's life. This is a threat that took place in the past and has caused a person to become unhealthy or unhappy. It will make life difficult as a person struggles to figure out how one's behaviors may be changed because of the trauma. Knowing how the trauma is produced helps to understand how this part of the human thinking pattern works. Traumas can happen in many ways and will more than likely happen without warning. It is through the sudden pains and worries produced by the trauma that it becomes harder for someone to carry on a normal life.

There are many types of trauma that someone could experience:

- Car accidents, sporting-related accidents, and many other accidents that cause injury can create trauma. The pains that came from being hurt could be too much for some people to bear.

- Medical-related problems do not have to be direct injuries. Traumas can occur when a person suffers from rare diseases or other issues that required extensive treatments, surgery, or hospitalization.

- Relational trauma is a situation where someone has problems with one's romantic or personal life. Common forms of relational trauma are abuse or neglect by a spouse.

- Natural disasters can cause traumas, such as an earthquake, hurricane, tornado, or something else that places one's sanity and safety in immediate jeopardy.

- Conditions relating to war can cause trauma, particularly those who are in the military or people from countries where war has been a persistent issue. People might see difficult or painful things in war or may be subject to harmful living conditions.

- Poverty is an issue that keeps people from being healthy or capable of managing their lives in a reasonable fashion. The trauma from poverty can increase when that person suffers poverty for a longer period of time.

- Adverse childhood events can make an impact. As the brain evolves, it becomes easier for a child to not fully understand what is happening during certain events. This could cause a child to feel emotionally distressed.

All of these problems can happen at any age, but they are issues that can create a great deal of emotional scarring. The impacts can be devastating and might be difficult for some people to recover. For instance, it might be a challenge for a person to get beyond a trauma due to the long-term effects or the ongoing dread that something like this could happen again. The fact that traumas can cause fears in many people based on what happened can directly influence what people might feel.

Effects of a Trauma

Trauma has many effects, although the specific problems produced will vary by each person:

- A person's safety may be threatened due to some trauma that occurred. That person could feel that the trauma might happen again.

- That someone's sanity may also be compromised. They might be afraid of what might happen and be emotionally scarred.

- The human body may also be impacted. Sometimes a trauma might cause long-term damage to the body or instill the fear that the damage could be permanent.

The problems that persist with trauma can be devastating and in some cases will last for one's lifetime. It is through the trauma that one experiences that it can become difficult for anyone to live a positive and controlled life.

The Value of Resiliency

Although trauma can be difficult to deal with, that does not mean that a person cannot recover from the trauma experienced. Resiliency refers to how well a person is capable of getting beyond the trauma to live comfortably. The human mind is resilient enough and a person will have a chance of recovering and move forward with one's life.

The things that can happen through resiliency are:

- Natural supports in one's life can be utilized to improve what one might be thinking and doing with life.

- People can do more things in their lives to help themselves. These include things that help people to be more proficient and productive in their lives while feeling positive about what they want to do for themselves.

- People can manage their feelings and keep them under control including looking into how those feelings are modulated and kept in check.

- There are always positive connections that can be made in one's life. These include connections that focus on how well one's life can be managed and kept positive.

- The most important thing is that a person will realize that he or she is worthy of life. This includes understanding that there are always things in the world for people to look forward to.

It is vital for people to look at what they are doing to be resilient and ready to respond to anything that happens.

Can Trauma Truly Be Erased?

As easy as it may be for the brain to manage trauma and recover, there are often times when it might be impossible for trauma to be erased completely. The greater concern is that the trauma that is produced might be deep and well-rooted in the mind. The threat involved can be dramatic depending on how intense the situation was and how long ago the trauma took place. The memories that surround the trauma are often difficult to repair. The worst part is that the effects of the trauma might remain throughout one's life.

For instance, a car wreck might have resulted in a permanent injury. A broken relationship might have led to someone feeling insecure. A major natural disaster might have caused the destruction of one's home. In other words, there is a chance that the trauma that is produced could be a challenge to manage, but it is through that worry that someone might be at risk of harm. The best thing that can be done for managing trauma is to work harder to find the root of the trauma and to address the fear that was a result. This is all about ensuring that the trauma of a situation can be kept under control and not be a threat to one's life.

Reframing the Trauma

There is always going to be some problem in one's life that will cause anxiety or fear to develop. A traumatic experience can cause anyone to feel fear, anger, grief, and sadness and can lead to a condition of PTSD. There comes a need to look at how the trauma evolved and what can be done to correct or soften the effects of the issue.

What Is Reframing?

Reframing is a process when someone looks at a certain situation from a new point of view. As the human mind changes, events and situations will be seen differently. Reframing is a way for someone to manage their emotions and thoughts. There are many ways a person can work toward reframing thoughts. Knowing how these issues are to be managed will help people understand their thinking and how their minds might function.

How Does the Trauma Help?

The first way to reframe the trauma is to see what meaning one might have put into the trauma. The key is to ask a basic question: "Why is this trauma important and how it is impacting my life?"

There are many possible answers:

- The trauma might have helped a person to reevaluate one's priorities. This includes developing a sudden revelation as to what is important to use in one's life in general.

- This trauma might also have created a change in one's mindset based on how much thinking was done to resolve certain problems caused by the trauma. New ways of thinking might have occurred with the possible goal of having corrected old and irrational ideas.

- An event may also make it easier for someone to have more confidence in other people. This could happen as other people would be there to help someone deal with difficulties that have happened. Knowing how to resolve these problems will allow a person to be more comfortable with what is happening in their life.

Here's an example. John had become fearful and depressed following his father's death in a workplace accident. John experienced a great deal of trauma as he feels unhappy and upset about his father's death because his father was so important in his life. The trauma that John experienced might have caused him to think very differently about his priorities in his life and what he wants to do. He might have recognized that he needs to change some of the ways he gets along with people. This includes deciding to be with his family members more often and to stop being such a slave to his work. He would have made this decision with the knowledge that life is short and that he needs to be with those he cares for more often than he has in the past.

Sometimes knowing how to handle one's life and get through some of the more difficult situations can change how someone feels and what they think is important in life. The trauma in one's life can help a person to reorganize one's life and appreciate what they are thankful for.

Chapter 17 – Repressed Memories - How to Access Them

As mentioned earlier, memories can develop fast and can become complex enough so that they sometimes might be lost due to decay or interference. There are also times when people might have memories that are hiding deep inside. These memories may be ones that a person does not have a full recollection of primarily because that person might have forgotten them. That person might be trying to intentionally keep those memories from coming out so that other people will not know they exist. A repressed memory is difficult to explore in the human mind. Such a memory is a past memory that a person has stored in the back of one's mind. Repressed memories have to be accessed by using cognitive psychology. A repressed memory is a recollection of a memory that is unconsciously blocked in one's mind. The block is due to the stress or trauma associated with the event in question.

For instance, a person might have a repressed memory of a violent action that took place. That person might have seen a violent attack in the past, but they have kept the memory in the back of their mind due to the fears that were produced by it. This memory over the violence is not something that is going to be pervasive in one's mind in a typical day. At the same time, the memory is not something that a person will recall. If anything, there would be no recognition of that memory for years in some cases.

This chapter includes details on not only how memories become repressed but also how they can be drawn out. By recovering those old memories, it becomes easier for someone to communicate with others and to talk openly about some of the worries or concerns that one might have about life in general.

Why a Memory Becomes Repressed

Although people try to keep their memories intact and strong, that does not mean every single memory will be kept and secured. The worst memories that a person might have will have to be protected. It does not take much for a memory to be repressed. The main reason why a person would develop a repressed memory is for protection. A repressed memory will protect a person from the harm that is often produced by the memory. The stresses that a person experiences in life as a result of such a difficult emotion should be minimal provided that the memory is hidden away and kept out of reach.

In addition, it is easier for people to protect themselves from many other feelings that might be harmful. When a memory is repressed, negative attitudes and anger can be prevented. In some cases, the memories are repressed because the person is unaware of what to do when trying to deal with the problems associated with negative memories. The brain tells a person that he or she is unable to handle the reality that comes with a negative experience. As a result, it is easier for the negative memory to be shielded and kept hidden. When negative memories cloud one's mind, it becomes easy for the brain to struggle and suffer from excess stress or anxiety. These worries make it harder for a person to function, thus leading to moving those memories into the back part of the brain. Forcing oneself into forgetting about these difficult memories is critical for managing one's life and keeping it from being too stressful. However, at the same time, this leads to significant problems regarding one's memories and a person's ability to manage those memories.

The Concern of Imagination Inflation

To understand how repressed memories may develop involves looking into imagination inflation and how this problem may come about in a person's mind over time. Sometimes a case of imagination inflation will happen as a result of the repressed memories that someone could have developed over time. By hiding those memories in one's mind, it becomes easier for a person to avoid facing some of the concerns regarding their fears. A person's imagination will become hard to manage after a while. The imaginary things that someone thinks about will make living harder and might cause beliefs to become unrealistic or difficult to comprehend.

The key is to allow the person who needs help with restoring an old memory to talk carefully about whatever it is they are trying to recall. The process of getting one's imagination in check is important as no one wants to bear with someone thinking about something that never took place no matter how vivid the memory might be.

How to Identify a Repressed Memory

The interesting thing about a repressed memory is that a person who has one might not know they have such a memory. That person might not fully recognize what is causing a fear to develop, but after finding that one has a repressed memory in some form, it becomes easier for that memory to be kept under control.

There are many ways a repressed memory can be identified:

1. A person might experience depression.

Depression is a common issue that people with repressed memories bear with. This could be having a memory that is causing a person to have consistent feelings of dread.

2. People with sleep disorders might have repressed memories.

People might not get to sleep as well due to their bodies being on high alert. They might be alert due to issues relating to those repressed memories. They might focus on what could happen in the future and the threats that can happen. These threats may come from the repressed memories one has. Someone with such memories might experience problems like struggling to fall asleep or stay asleep. People who suffer from restless sleep episodes or those who wake up feeling tired might have such disorders as well. These episodes should be persistent and not just one-off occasions for them to be seen as threats to one's health.

3. People might be hesitant to talk about some of the things in their past.

Past events are often difficult for people to manage if they are very negative. Those events will be hidden in one's mind long and they will try to avoid certain emotions or worries surrounding those negative memories.

How Can These Memories Be Recovered?

To treat a person's fears through cognitive psychology, it is critical to go through a person's repressed memories. This includes knowing how to reach the memories that one is hiding. Cognitive psychology may be used to assist in recovering such a memory. After the memory is gathered and reviewed, it can be analyzed and inspected. Knowing how to get into these memories is vital for helping a person to have a stronger life without worries getting in the way.

1. The first thing to do is to examine a person's life story. Start by talking about the earliest personal events that someone might recall.

To do this, a simple notebook can be used with a timeline layout. A timeline may be produced to illustrate what has happened from the past to today. Gathering information on all of these personal events helps to create connections. A person might start to lose track of certain memories at some point in their life. Let's talk about an example. John would be asked to talk about all the things that have happened in his life. He can talk about the places he lived, where he went to school, the jobs he has worked, and so forth.

2. Review the types of events that took place in someone's life. Look at how they link and how much a person recalls about certain events.

For instance, a person might state that his or her parents divorced at a certain point in time. The next few years might be seen as a blur. This could be a sign that the divorce had something to do with the problems that one has. In John's case, he might talk about how he had a difficult time in life due to a traumatic event that took place. His memories would start to change and be not very detailed due to such an event.

3. Pay attention to any events that might be traumatic.

The traumatic events are the ones that cause repressed memories to occur. The difficulties that came about within one's life might be points that could have caused a person to change and become a little harder to stay emotionally stable.

For instance, John might be talking with someone about how his brother died when he was ten years old. John might start to hide details about his family life from that point onward. This might be a suggestion that he is afraid of facing certain events relating to his family. Perhaps he has a fear of commitments or attachment.

4. Focus on the timeframe that the traumatic events took place. Talk about what caused that person to have such difficult memories.

In John's case, it would help to talk with him about his life before his brother's death and then right after. He should be asked about any changes he went through and the changes that came along in his life. All those changes in his life might suggest that he has fears that came from that time period.

5. Ask about any actions that someone might have taken around that time period.

All of those feelings during a traumatic period might cause certain feelings to develop. These include general aversions and fears. After a while, John might talk about how he recalls not wanting to get on public transportation after his brother died. This could be a sign of how this type of service had something to do with his brother's death. Maybe he died in a wreck involving a transportation service or he was hit by a transit vehicle and killed. At this point, it becomes easier to notice that John is afraid of public transit and that he has been hiding his fears of the service because of the bad things that happened to him involving it as a child. He might try to avoid such a service. By talking with him further, it begins to become clear that he could become nervous about some past feelings.

The repressed memory should have been fully retrieved at this point. The source of the fear will be revealed so the subject can be treated. The next stage in cognitive psychology, the stage relating to treating a fear, can take place at this juncture. The most important thing about repressed memories is that no one should try to rush these memories into the forefront. It takes a bit of effort and discussion to help understand what a person is afraid of through such memories. By unraveling the mystery, a solution may be found.

An Authenticity Warning

There is one dramatic concern that must be considered regarding how repressed memories may develop. This point refers to how authentic some of the repressed memories one has might be. Although a person might be detailed and specific regarding some of these memories, it would be next to impossible to decide precisely how accurate those memories actually are. The repressed memories one has might be deep in the mind to the point where it is hard for them to reappear accurate and detailed.

The greatest concern is that those memories could be ones that a person might have just thought about out of the blue. It is hard to determine if those memories are true because they have been trapped in one's mind for such a long time. Although the repressed memories might help and be easy to use to determine what someone is feeling, it can be difficult to recognize if those memories are accurate or fictional.

Chapter 18 – How Cognitive Behavioral Therapy Controls Fears

The crippling effects and issues that can come with fears can prove to be difficult for anyone to live with. Cognitive psychology can help control fears once they have been identified. As a person's fears are analyzed, their mental issues can be treated.

Realistic Thinking

One point of cognitive psychology to manage fears is thinking realistically. Sometimes the fears a person exhibits might be based on unrealistic or outlandish beliefs. For instance, a person might be afraid of flying in an airplane because of the worry that the engines will stop working or something will break apart while in the air. A person has to think realistically. Many fears develop because a person does not think realistically about what is involved. A person might not be aware that an airplane is durable and is constructed to stay intact in any conditions while in the air. However, many people become afraid of flying because they do not understand how a plane works. Knowing the truth about something and what might happen can help alleviate fears. There are several steps that may be used to cognitively think about the problems that one has:

1. Analyze the certain issues surrounding a fear.

2. Look for information relating to the item one is afraid of.

3. Find connections between the fear and what can be done to resolve the issue.

4. After looking at the connections, it becomes easier to understand the truth about what someone might be afraid of.

This strategy is vital for people who have significant fears that are based on outlandish thinking. For instance, a person who is afraid of dogs out of the fear that they might attack will discover through training and analysis that any memories one might have had of dogs attacking could be based on unrealistic values or ideas and not reality.

Create Challenges to Negative Thoughts

Realistic thinking is helpful, but one way to go a step further is to produce cognitive challenges. Attempting to change one's cognition over certain fears requires an effort to determine what one might be thinking at a certain time. There are a few steps that can be used to challenge some of the negative things that one might be thinking about:

1. Look at the fortune-telling actions one engages in.

Many people link certain fears to the fortunes they tell themselves. For instance, a person might not want to touch a dog due to the belief that the dog will attack. The challenge, in this case, is to think about what will happen when someone pets a dog. The dog might not respond harshly when it is petted. The dog will instead feel happy and pleased that someone is giving it attention. The fortune that someone told at the start might end up being false. By getting into a realistic situation with something, a person will discover that whatever was being done earlier is not something that someone has to be worried or fearful about.

2. Review overgeneralizations.

One part of improper cognitive thinking is people making generalizations. For example, a person might have petted a dog and thinks that the rash they developed later was caused by that petting action. The truth is that the rash might have come from something else and not from the dog at all.

    3. Think about the catastrophes that someone might consider possible.

Catastrophes are problems that people get into when they overthink. For instance, a person might think that when a person coughs while on an airplane that they might have Ebola or some other deadly or dangerous condition.

    4. Develop a plan to manage a fear.

Knowing what to do to control the fear is important. This can include having extra exposure to the stimuli that one is afraid of. Anyone who can handle a fear the right way will have a better chance at moving forward in life.

Preparing Self-Statements

Fears are often easier to control when a person is ready to express one's true self with a series of self-statements that are positive or confident in nature. For instance, a person might say, "I am a smart person" or "I know what to do in certain situations that might happen."

The process for producing self-statements and using them to manage the fears one holds will entail:

    1. Think about something positive in one's life.

    2. Review the cases where certain fears might happen.

3. Recall the positive self-statement that was produced. Make the statement relevant to the fear.

4. Keep focusing on that statement and recognize how it applies to the fear.

5. As the mind becomes more comfortable, the fear will be minimized.

A good example of this is dealing with a fear of motorcycles. A person might be afraid of motorcycles because getting on one might be too risky. They might be afraid of slipping while on a motorcycle or something flying into one's body and causing serious physical harm. A positive self-statement to use would be, "I am an alert person" or "I am very careful wherever I go." These statements reinforce the fact that there's nothing to be worried about and that he or she is careful.

As the self-statement is repeated, the person who gets on the motorcycle will feel a little more comfortable. The positivity that comes from one's mind will crowd out the negative thoughts. The statements can be remembered and restated whenever that person starts to feel nervous once again. After a while, the self-statements will not be necessary. The fear will not be as strong as the person will be used to the experience. In this situation, the person will know that the motorcycle one is on is much safer than what had been assumed it would have been and they will no longer have that fear. The self-statements need to be realistic, relevant, and easy to recall.

Additional Questions to Ask

When considering the negative thoughts one has that might cause a fear to develop, questions can be asked such as:

1. What evidence contradicts the thoughts one has?

This relates to realistic thinking. For instance, a person might say that he or she does not want to get on an airplane due to that plane being too dangerous. However, evidence shows that millions of people fly on airplanes and there are thousands of flights that take off and land with no problems each day. Even personal evidence may be considered. A person might notice that one's friends have gone on planes many times and they did so safely.

2. What can be done to control any problems that might occur?

Many safeguards may be used to resolve any worries or problems one might have surrounding a fear. For instance, an airplane has many safety mechanisms that help to keep the vehicle operating in the air safely. Regular mandatory maintenance routines are also important to note.

3. How long might it take for the fear in question to be fully resolved?

People should not try to rush the process. It can take weeks or even months to conquer a fear. The key is to allow the process of managing a fear or other worry to happen naturally. Asking enough questions about a fear helps to challenge the concerns that one has.

Chapter 19 – Using the Fear Ladder For Managing Intense Fears

Another way to use cognitive psychology to manage fears is to look at the situations that might surround a fear. How a person perceives situations will impact how someone develops a fear. A way to manage those fears through perception is working with a fear ladder. The method of using realistic thinking focuses on debunking myths and beliefs that cause fears and the fear ladder concentrates directly on getting in touch with those fears. By getting into regular contact with the fears someone has, it becomes easier for that person to be less afraid of something. The perceptions a person has will be less threatening and possibly easier to manage.

A Progressive Approach

The fear ladder is designed as an exposure-based form of therapy to manage fears and other negative concerns. The important thing about the ladder is that it is a progressive approach to resolving one's fears. The fear ladder is used to conquer dangerous fears that might be emotionally crippling. The fear ladder investigates the smallest bits of detail about one's fear to resolve them gradually.

Intense fears take a little longer for people to resolve. Being able to get those emotional worries kept in check is crucial to one's life and one's ability to have a healthier emotional attitude. Even the most difficult fears can be resolved if enough effort is put into the process of getting the fear kept under control.

How to Produce the Fear Ladder

The fear ladder can be produced and eventually conquered by using four steps:

1. Start by making a list of any fearful concerns.

For instance, a person who is afraid of flying might list various problems including issues like the sounds of an airplane, the cramped spaces inside a plane, the security process for boarding a plane, and the risk of one's luggage or other items being lost while in transit. Even the flight attendant reading the safety instructions might be a worry.

2. Produce a fear ladder by organizing those concerns based on what is the most fearful versus the least worrisome.

For instance, the least frightening part of getting on a plane might be going through airport security. After that, there is the worry about being cramped inside a tight space. In this case, a person will progressively move toward the worst fear by working with the smallest worries and then moving up to the greatest fears.

The fear ladder can include as many rungs as needed. They must be placed in a logical order.

3. Start working up the ladder.

The least fearful thing should be conquered first to help a person deal with the fears one by one. For flying, the person would start by going through airport security. That person could travel to an airport to learn about how the security system works. This could help to understand that the security process is easy to handle. Next, the person can investigate what it is like inside a plane. The safeguards that are used in the plane can then be discussed followed by what types of sounds are produced as a plane takes off, flies, and lands.

> 4. The person should practice climbing up the ladder when possible. That person should not try to rush one's way up the ladder.

It is imperative for a person to be gentle and cautious when going up the ladder to deal with each progressive part of the fear. When that person is conditioned, prepared, and is ready to get on a plane, that person can eventually enjoy a pleasant experience on a plane. As a result of the efforts involved with the fear ladder, that person will no longer be afraid of flying. This can take a bit of time to complete, but after a while, that person will feel better about one's ability to get on a plane and to enjoy it.

Those who work with a fear ladder will start to perceive things in a new way. The added exposure and comfort that comes with what someone had feared will allow that fear to be resolved. This is critical for those whose fears might keep them from having the fun that they deserve.

An Example of the Fear Ladder

To fully understand how well the fear ladder works when conquering fears, it helps to look at this example. Jeff is afraid of cats because he feels they might claw and hurt him. He feels that they might trigger difficult allergies as well. By developing a fear ladder, Jeff can learn that cats are not animals that he should be afraid of. He would make a list of things that he is afraid of surrounding cats and find ways to manage his worries about them.

1. To start, Jeff can look at pictures of cats to see what they are like. He can notice that they are not as harmful as he has thought.

2. Jeff would then watch videos of cats in action. It is clear that there are plenty of cat videos, but he can use these videos to notice that they are not harmful and that they can be completely harmless.

3. Jeff would then start to get closer to cats. He could look at one through a window. He might even see that cat look back at him with curiosity.

4. He would then stand a little closer to a cat. He can stay a few feet away from a cat, but after a while, he will get closer to the point where he could pet the cat.

5. Jeff can pet the cat and notice that the cat is not going to harm him.

6. After a while, Jeff could possibly pick up a cat and give it a pet.

As Jeff works to manage his fear, he will start to notice that there is nothing to worry about surrounding cats. He will feel better around them and know that his perceptions surround cats were false. The cats he may come across will not be dangerous or harmful to him in any way. It is critical that he avoids rushing the process. A person who works through the fear ladder should be doing so at one's own pace so the risks will be limited and kept under control. A person can skip steps on the fear ladder, but this might be risky for some. Continuing with a prepared pattern for going along the ladder may be the safest bet.

How Many Steps?

The fear ladder can have as many steps as one wishes to incorporate into the process. Having enough steps on the ladder ensures one will have a clear idea how to progressively get past the fear. A person should review the intensity of the fear and everything that surrounds that fear. The total number of rungs on the fear ladder can vary based on the intensity of the situation and the fears produced. There are no limits as to how many steps may be placed on the fear ladder. The person who devises the ladder should at least be careful not to have too many rungs so that it would be next to impossible to resolve the fear in question.

How Much Time?

It is up to the person who is trying to resolve a fear to determine how long it should take. Having a plan for keeping that fear from being a problem will surely take a bit of time, but it at least helps a person to be prepared and ready to feel comfortable with what they are doing when trying to manage the issues. Those who work hard to manage their fears will feel stronger and more confident in their abilities to handle any difficult situations that they might experience.

Chapter 20 – Exposure Therapy to Control Smaller Fears

One strategy for managing fears that deserves its own chapter is Exposure Therapy. As the name suggests, this focuses on exposing people to stimuli that they are afraid of. This practice is to help a person feel more confident with particular stimuli and to realize that the fears someone might have are not really concerning or realistic. Exposure therapy has been used as a cognitive psychology procedure that works well for people struggling with post-traumatic stress disorder or PTSD. It may also be used by those who have exceptional fears and need assistance with getting over them.

Exposure Therapy Differs From the Fear Ladder

On the surface, Exposure Therapy sounds like it could be similar to the fear ladder, but there are two differences between the two. First, the fear ladder focuses on many aspects that are part of a fear and what can be done to resolve the concerns someone has. Exposure therapy focuses on direct contact with something.

Second, Exposure Therapy is designed with minor fears in mind. The fear ladder focuses on being more progressive in handling the fears one has developed. With the Exposure Therapy process, a fear is directly targeted and analyzed to see how the issues or concerns may be corrected. Exposure therapy is often paired with relaxation exercises. The key is to link such exercises with the exposure to something one is afraid of. The goal is to allow the brain to relax and to stop feeling stress surrounding a certain concern.

Think of Exposure Therapy as though it was the opposite of the Watson experiment mentioned earlier in this guide. Whereas Watson found that fears can be linked to traumatic happenings, Exposure Therapy shows that fears can be resolved by conditioning the mind to perceive something more peaceful and comforting instead of fearful. This does not mean that this should be used in lieu of the fear ladder. If anything, both the practices in this chapter and the functions of the fear ladder should be used to help someone to manage the worries and issues one might develop.

How to Enter Into Exposure Therapy

The process for using Exposure Therapy should be rather basic and should not be too complicated:

1. Start by observing the specific thing that one is afraid of.

Let's go back to the airport example from the previous chapter. A person might be afraid of flying, but at the same time, the experience is not as intensive as it could be. The only thing a person might be afraid of is what might happen during the takeoff and landing process.

2. Learn more about the thing that triggers the fear.

The person in this situation can learn more about the takeoff and landing procedures. The process should be studied based on the parts used to get the plane to move and how it will be propelled into the air. The information will help the person be prepared for whatever might happen.

3. Experience the fear firsthand by observing it from afar.

Watching a plane take off or land can help a person determine the process. This exposure makes it easier for someone to notice that nothing fearful happens. The person can watch videos of planes taking off and landing, but it might be better if a person observes the planes taking off and landing directly from an observation deck at a local airport. This can help someone feel more confident in the planes' ability to take off and land.

4. After being exposed to the fearful item and learning more, a person can take that next step and have access to the item that one had feared for so long.

The person who was afraid of flying can get onto the plane and eventually go on a flight. That someone will feel more confident in knowing how the takeoff and landing processes work.

How to Tell If the Fear Is Too Intense

Exposure therapy does well for fears that are not too extreme. In some cases, it might help to notice how intense one's fear might be. Using the fear ladder might be a better option for those who are too fearful. There are a few things to notice when considering at a fear and deciding if Exposure Therapy is best or if the fear ladder should be used instead. These points are as follows:

- Look at how many parts surround the fear including observing that the fear has more than just one or two small details.

In the case of flying, a person might be afraid of the takeoff and landing process and nothing else. This means that someone can use Exposure Therapy to become relaxed. Meanwhile, a person who fears every aspect of flying including the security control might need the fear ladder to handle all the issues.

- Analyze how strong the fears might be based on one's attitude. A person might have a very extreme fear if that person refuses to talk about it.

A person who refuses to believe that there is a problem might need help through the fear ladder to progressively see what the problems in a situation might be

- Review the intensity of the fear based on how long someone has had the fear. A person who has had a fear for a longer period of time might benefit more from the fear ladder.

Using the fear ladder is best in cases where someone's fears might be too extreme or hard to control. Those who have sudden fears that just happened might find success using Exposure Therapy.

Calming Exercises for Exposure Therapy

The process of calming the body and mind during Exposure Therapy is critical. Sometimes a person might become overwhelmed in the process. This requires a person to develop a plan for keeping the mind under control. Calming exercises are more prominent in the earliest stages of Exposure Therapy when a person is not used to what is causing the fear. Added support for one's mind to keep from feeling too much emotional stress or worry is vital.

Several things can be done to relax during this process:

1. Concentrate on breathing. Try to keep the breathing regulated.

The breathing should be properly synchronized without the breathing sounding intense.

2. Go for a little walk if possible.

A gentle walk is often good enough for calming the mind. Walking along in a peaceful forested or park area is great as it gives a person the opportunity to relax and focus on the trees and other natural surroundings. The key is to allow the brain to relax so it can feel restored and ready to take in whatever needs to be explored when it is time to work toward managing one's fear.

3. Focus on the senses.

The human senses are powerful and help control the mind to deal with stress and turmoil.

- Look at things that might be pleasing to the eyes.

- Smell something gentle and relaxing in a space. This could be a nice decorative candle placed somewhere in a room or even the clean air outside.

- Enjoy a cup of tea or coffee or something else that tastes good. Drink it slowly.

- Pay attention to some of the natural sounds in an area, whether the birds in a park, the rustling of nearby trees, or the soft sound of music.

How Often to Exercise?

The Exposure Therapy exercise should work as often as one wants. It is also important that the exercise is done at a pace someone is comfortable with. The Exposure Therapy exercise works best when planned with enough time in mind. Anyone who tries to rush the exercise could be at risk of keeping the effort from working. It is through persistence and patience that a person can use this to cognitively manage one's fear.

Exposure therapy practice focuses mainly on making it easier for someone to feel confident about how one's fear can be controlled. Exposure to something one is afraid of is helpful to create a direct cognitive link that focuses on understanding what causes the fear. A person's thinking about something may also be challenged as anything unrealistic or questionable would be resolved as well.

Chapter 21 – Exposure and Response Prevention – A Solution For OCD-Related Fears

The ERP or Exposure and Response Prevention plan works well for managing obsession compulsive disorder or OCD, and may also manage fears.

A Focus on OCD Fears

Obsessive compulsive disorder or OCD is a mental condition where someone experiences several obsessions that lead to compulsive behaviors. A person will engage in behaviors out of the fear that something wrong might happen. OCD causes people to be afraid of many situations if they do not complete certain actions. Let's consider the situation of Tom and how he might use the same repetitive actions while in the bathroom. As he gets into the bathroom, he might turn on the faucet when he gets in out of the fear that someone might listen to him while in the bathroom. This OCD trigger occurs as he tries to keep other people from hearing him for whatever reason.

As unusual and potentially wasteful as it might be for him to turn on the faucet, he will do this whenever he goes into a bathroom. This might worsen so that he does not want to use public restrooms even if he really has a need for using the bathroom. He would avoid using the restroom because he knows that there are strangers in the area. Also, he might be afraid of cases where the sink just shuts off automatically after a few seconds; this would keep it from running all the time, so he can be quickly identified as being in the bathroom.

Any kind of obsession could cause someone to have worries. For instance, a person might be focused on organizing the pencils and pens on their desk in a very specific layout. When those utensils are shifted or not aligned properly, that person immediately becomes fearful and will do anything to correct the issue. OCD is a frustrating issue. CBT can assist in keeping the OCD that one has from becoming worse. It is critical to first look at the fear has and how this problem might be organized and controlled before it can become an obsession.

Get to Know a Fear

Recognize and understand the fear that one has. In Tom's case, his fear is that he is worried about people paying attention to him while he is in the bathroom.

1. Start by thinking about the obsessions that one might have.

In Tom's case, he is obsessed with thinking that people are going to hear him in the bathroom.

2. Look at the triggers that cause the fear to become intense.

Refer to the trigger section from earlier for further details. Tom might have triggers like noticing that a bathroom is large enough so that people might directly notice him.

3. Find out how long the fear has lasted. How long ago did the fear appear?

Sometimes the fear might be something that has persisted for years, or maybe it is a new fear.

For Tom, he might have developed OCD a few years earlier following an embarrassing situation in his life. Maybe he just started to be worried about his use of the bathroom.

Planning a Chart

A chart can be made by someone with OCD to record information on when and how an OCD-related fear was triggered.

1. Write down the date that the fear began or was first noticed.

2. Write the triggers for an obsession.

The trigger should be something that caused the fear to develop. Tom might write that it was triggered by a faucet not staying on after it was activated. This might have made him worried because he cannot complete the routine that he feels a need to manage.

3. The obsession that was triggered by the second step should be listed.

In most cases, Tom's OCD obsession will happen as a result of his need to use the sink while in the bathroom. He must explain the problem that he has based on the feelings that were produced through his repeated actions.

4. Write down on a scale of 0 to 10 the intensity of the fear.

Not all OCD attacks are going to be intense. A ranking should be used to determine how strong the fear is.

5. Any coping strategies that were used should be included.

Many people who have OCD-related fears will do what they can to resolve those worries that they might have. Tom might have tried to cope with his worries by rushing through a bathroom use as quickly as possible. This chart can have as many entries as one wants. Tom can use this chart to help him figure out how he is using the bathroom and what he needs to do to keep from being nervous in certain situations. More importantly, he will start to look at the chart and notice what is causing him to feel a certain way. At this point, Tom might look at what he could do to resolve the fear and keep it from being far too intense.

Working With the Fear Ladder

Exposure therapy can help at this next point, but it may be even better to work with the fear ladder. With the fear ladder, it will be easier for a mental problem to be resolved and controlled before it can become worse. For Tom, he can use the chart that he produced to get an idea of what things might be the most intense triggers of his OCD actions. Whatever the weakest trigger was will be the bottom rung of his fear ladder.

Managing a Fear With OCD

Although the points in this chapter are useful for anyone to use when managing a fear even when one has OCD, there are a few considerations to look at. A person who has OCD might have a harder time using CBT processes to handle fears:

1. Find a way to resist urges to complete a compulsion.

People with OCD often have a need to complete their compulsive behaviors before doing anything else. The key of ERP and CBT is to manage fears without falling for those compulsions. It is perfectly fine if a person with OCD fails to follow this step the first couple of times. Trial and error might be a necessity to follow when aiming to manage significant concerns relating to one's emotional processes.

2. Be willing to ask for help if necessary.

Sometimes it helps to ask for some outside help to manage certain problems in one's life. A person with OCD should be willing to ask for help to manage certain emotional problems. This can work well when managing the emotions or struggles that someone might endure.

3. It might help to delay any compulsions at the beginning.

The best thing to do in this situation is to wait a few minutes before acting on a compulsion. Instead of acting on it right away, and eventually extending the amount of time before acting on the compulsion.

4. Be willing to engage in re-exposure if the process does not fully work.

Re-exposure is when a person will expose oneself to the triggering situation, again and again, trying to resist performing the compulsive behavior. The goal is to get through the same situation without the compulsive action.

5. Never judge one's fear.

It is true that OCD-based fears are a little more unusual than others. To some, these fears are extremely irrational and in some cases silly. The fears are indeed real, and no one should judge a person based on the fear that one might be showing. Instead, it is best to accept a person and the action they are doing. Talking with that person about the issue and using metacognition to determine what they might think about the problem they have is helpful. ERP is a unique process that works well for people who need extra help to manage the difficult concerns they have. This works well for people with OCD as it assists them with managing some of the emotional problems that might make it harder for someone to get through a situation without performing obsessive actions.

Chapter 22 – Replacing Stimuli

Different stimuli can be exchanged to try and resolve fears and other issues. The process of replacing stimuli can help people associate what they are afraid of with other things. For instance, John might be afraid of and he might associate a dog with violence. In this case, John would try to associate something other than violence with a dog. The stimulus of violent images or thoughts would be replaced with something positive like an image of a sunny field. The key is to get John to realize that dogs can be associated with positive rather than negative thoughts. This lets John feel comfortable around a dog and will not result in him being worried about being near a dog.

Although this sounds like a simple strategy for managing one's fears, the process is more complicated. The CBT approach could take weeks or even months to complete. When used right, a person can start to associate a fear with something new. A few basic steps will make the process work:

1. Review the stimulus that causes the fear or anxiety attack to develop.

Focus on the emotional triggers and feelings that stimulate the cause of a fear.

2. Determine how negative feelings are produced based on the stimulus presented.

Having some control over the thoughts helps keep the problems one has from being a significant threat.

3. Identify things that might produce positive feelings.

Anyone can be stimulated by positive items or attitudes. The goal is to keep the issues that one has from being more of a burden than necessary.

    4. Find a way to incorporate positive stimuli into one's mind.

The positive thought can be used the next time a triggering event happens. Instead of thinking of one's original thought, the new stimulus may be used. This allows a person to feel more confident and in control. This process is flexible and allows a person to decide on the stimulus with which one wishes to replace an old thought.

An Example

Here's an example of replacing a stimulus. Keith is trying to manage his fear of rainy days. He often has worries about how rain is going to make it harder for him to do anything outdoors. He may also be afraid of flooding or other problems. His mind will respond to a rainfall event by thinking about the bad things that could happen. The stimuli, in this case, may be the feeling that the roads are going to flood, his basement will flood, and his lawn will die. With the right moves, he can get rid of the stimuli.

To replace the stimuli of flooding, Keith will start to focus on something like a rainbow forming or his lawn not becoming too dry. He will use these stimuli to notice that the things that come after a rainfall are always beautiful and that his lawn will not die because it is getting the proper hydration it requires. When the next rainfall event happens, Keith will start to think about the rainfall and the healthy lawn that will grow from the rain. He might have struggled with thinking about floods, but over time, Keith will start to use the new stimuli to keep him from being too obsessed with the potential for his basement to flood or his lawn to die. It will take time for him to get used to this, but after a while, Keith will start to notice that it is not too hard to think of the positive things rain brings.

How Long Does It Take to Respond To the New Stimuli?

The process required to manage the new stimuli is simple, but it takes some time for the mind to get used to the situation. This might be determining how much work would be needed to memorize the stimuli. It should be easier to respond to stimuli when they are relevant to the event. People should expect to give this process of replacing stimuli a few tries before it can be effective. Knowing how those thoughts occur should make it easier for someone to think about what one might be doing about one's attitudes or thoughts.

Chapter 23 – Socratic Questioning to Curtail Irrational Thinking

Many of the fears that people develop are the result of the irrational thoughts. Sometimes what someone thinks about a fear is not realistic at all. Challenging irrational thinking should focus on cognitive restructuring. Restructuring helps organize one's thoughts. Socratic questioning is a concept used to help uncover issues that someone has. The goal of this questioning is to find the reasons why certain fears are produced and to explore how irrational those thoughts and worries are.

Socratic questioning is a practice that was first introduced by Socrates, the iconic philosopher of the fifth century BC. He found answers by asking questions of his students. He believed that the best way to find ideas and to understand what people might think is to ask questions. By doing so, the validity of those questions or other concerns can be unraveled. The method works with the assumption that the person who is being asked the questions has a mindset where one is not fully aware of a situation or how it might develop. The student will learn through questioning the things they do and do not understand. More importantly, the procedure helps students to question what they learn and to be more introspective in what they want to do with their lives.

How does Socratic questioning curtail the irrational thoughts that cause certain fears to develop? To illustrate Socratic questioning, we will discuss Pat who is thinking about how she is able to complete a task in the accounting office where she works. Pat might think that the task is too complicated and she will not be able to manage the task. This produces the fear that she could fail because she would not get everything done on time and that any efforts to try and finish the task on time would result in her rushing things and fail. By using Socratic questioning, Pat will eventually notice that she doesn't have to struggle with emotional issues or problems relating to the work she is trying to complete. She would find that there is no need to fear the task she is attempting to complete.

1. Create a thought that has to be questioned.

The thought should be about what to do to resolve certain problems. At this point, Pat would say "I have a major client that needs a project completed in two weeks, but there is no way I can do it. I am afraid that I will fail because I have no idea how to get this task completed." This thought is something she could question to try and give herself the motivation she needs to complete that task within the timeframe.

2. Review the evidence that goes toward the thought versus the evidence that counters it.

Pat would list that the arguments supporting her thought: there is only so much time in the day for her to work on the project and it is highly detailed. She might feel as though the process involved would be too extensive and difficult for her to handle. This, in turn, makes it harder for her to determine what she can do to resolve the problem and complete the task. Then Pat would argue that she has done tasks like this before and that she understands the steps associated with the task in question. She might also notice that there are many things she can do to complete the task quickly if she gets help from others in the same office. The main goal of this process is to make the points as even as possible. It would be even better if Pat knew how to get the evidence against her negative view to overwhelm the evidence that confirms what she fears the most.

3. Look at what the evidence is based on. Are the details based on facts or feelings?

This is a self-explanatory question. Sometimes the problems one has are only in the mind. There has to be evidence to support that a person is capable of doing the task or at least evidence to prove that a negative thought is wrong. Pat might find evidence suggesting that she has done several complicated accounting tasks in the past and that she should not have trouble to finish another task. However, her original thought to be questioned might be based on her feelings. She might think that her task at hand is going to be too difficult for her to manage and that she is too tired from lots of work that she has already completed.

4. Is this a black and white thought, or is there a way for the thinking process to be more extensive?

A black and white thought is one that is only the most positive or negative aspects of something. When this type of thought occurs, a person is not thinking about all the things that could take place in a situation. A thought that is black and white might be more complicated or detailed than what one might think. It is up to the thinker to consider the in-depth details that go into the question. Pat should ask herself more about that initial thought to see if it is really hard for her to get a good answer to her question. She needs to look into whether or not there is a hidden meaning to the question that she is asking or if it can be directly answered. Knowing what she is asking and how she can get the situation under control is vital to her success.

5. Look at the assumptions that could have been made about the thought.

The assumptions are what someone assumes will happen. Pat might assume that the task will be complicated, but maybe she has not read the details of the task and see the specific work that she would have to complete.

6. What interpretations would other people have about the same thought?

Pat might ask other people at the accounting firm about the task. They can share their thoughts with Pat to let her know what makes a task valuable or unique in their eyes.

7. What evidence is being used to bolster the thought?

Any evidence used to support a thought might be a result of one's personal attitudes. Sometimes the evidence might just support the initial thought. There has to also be evidence that goes in the opposite direction to prove that whatever someone is doing is not that hard to follow or use. Pat should discover if there are any bits of evidence that counteract her original thought. She might have evidence from prior projects suggesting that a similar client that she had to work for was extremely complicated. There might also be evidence suggesting that the details the new client has sent are not as difficult to use as the last client. By reviewing every bit of evidence, including the content that counters Pat's original argument, it becomes easier for her to have a plan to manage her work.

8. Is there something about the beliefs one has that could be interpreted as an exaggeration?

Sometimes the thoughts are general exaggerations of what someone could be thinking. Exaggerations are commonplace in some dire situations. When a person is suffering from pressure or stress, they will start to think that only bad things are going to happen. It is through further analysis that it could turn out the issue may not be difficult. Pat has to take a more realistic approach to her thought at this time. She has to see that the fear she has could be an exaggeration.

9. Is the thought being produced out of habit?

Fears often come from habits. People just assume that one thing can be felt for any situation one enters into. By using Socratic questioning, a person can become introspective and capable of thinking about the habits they have developed. Pat might have a regular habit of assuming the worst when she is given new tasks. By looking at her fears, Pat might start to notice that the things she is worried about are not as difficult as she might think they were. Pat would have to see if any facts support her thought. If there are no thoughts to support it, this must mean that she is producing this idea from habit.

10. Did someone create this thought? Is the person who created this thought related to the self?

Pat might think about when she first experienced such a thought as this. There is a chance that maybe someone else in the workplace might have told her something and that caused her to be fearful.

11. What is the most likely scenario being produced in this situation?

Is the scenario being produced in this situation realistic? Is the thinking too frustrating or outlandish to be taken seriously? This would lead to the scenario being analyzed being controlled a little more without problems.

The Overall Goal

A person needs to understand the truth behind what they are thinking or feeling. As it might turn out, the fears or worries that someone might develop could be a whole lot of nothing. As Socratic questioning takes place, the mind will start to notice how unrealistic a thought is. This opens up the mind to recognize that the situation at hand is safe to pursue. This can be ideal for managing fears, but it can also work for any worries or other emotional concerns one might have.

A Secondary Socratic Approach for Private Concerns

Socratic questioning may be used for any purpose, but this works best in cases where someone might think about negative issues. There is a potential that Socratic questioning may help to keep those negative attitudes from being too great a burden to manage. There are often cases where a person might have an issue that is private in nature and cannot be brought out to the public. Such specific situations are among the toughest ones for people to manage, but Socratic questioning can still help with resolving those issues. In fact, the questioning process, in this case, will be a little shorter in duration and complexity than when trying to resolve problems with the help of others.

The process does well with managing negative issues by helping a person find something good in an issue. It has been widely believed by people throughout the years that there is always some kind of silver lining that comes with a dark cloud. That is, something positive has to be found out of the negative situations. This is an optimist's philosophy. A tenet of cognitive psychology is that negative events need to be replaced with positive ones. This includes taking negative thoughts and adding new positive ones.

A minimized version of Socratic questioning can be used for basic thoughts that do not require procedures or help from other people. The results can be effective in any situation. Note that this process works best in cases where the emotional or mental issues one has are not strong.

How to Do It

The process to take the negatives and make them into positives is not challenging. However, it does require a little more effort. The number of questions in this form of Socratic questioning will be fewer than what would be asked during the more traditional version of this practice. This is a simplified approach.

1. Write down a negative thought that one might have.

The first point is to write down something that one is worried about or is not happy with. The person must be direct about this without fabricating things. Everything must be listed even if the content in question is difficult. For this example, let us talk about Colin and how he is worried about his debts. He owes too much money to credit card companies and student loans. In this case, he might say, "I have too much debt and I don't think I will ever resolve it any time soon."

2. Look at the evidence that supports the thought.

In Colin's case, he might notice that his bank account is too small to handle all his debts at once.

3. Review the evidence that contradicts the thought.

Added research may be required in this process, but this part of Socratic questioning requires more introspection and an analysis of one's private or personal issues to get an idea of what someone is thinking. Colin would have to look at how he has been managing his debts so far. He might notice that he has managed to reduce the total amount of debt that he owes, thus making it slightly easier to pay it off versus what it might have been earlier. Therefore, he is already making progress by questioning the validity of his negative statement.

4. Are there are real potentials that may be used?

For Colin, he would state that he will continue to work to get the funds he needs to pay off those debts. Having enough work is vital for him as it becomes easier for him to cover the issues that he has, thus improving his emotions. As he puts this thought into consideration, it becomes clear to him that it should not be hard for him to resolve the problems he has with his debts. This process for Socratic questioning is much shorter, but it is a practice that works best for those who need help answering questions without asking other people or where it would be difficult to get input from others.

Being able to take the negative things and turn them into positives does not have to be too complicated. The process that one uses for taking negatives and finding positives can be used regularly to resolve the mental issues that one might develop and struggle with.

Should Other People Be Consulted Anyway?

It is optional for a person to ask for additional help from another person when having a problem resolved in this fashion. Although minimized Socratic questioning works well in this situation, it may help to ask for outside help depending on how serious the issue is. This includes situations of depression, fears of trivial items, or even cases where one's financial or physical security might be in jeopardy.

Chapter 24 – Understanding Anxiety

Anxiety is a feeling of worry or being uneasy about something that might develop in life. This includes worries about something that will happen in the future that a person is not fully certain or confident will actually happen. All people feel nervous at various points in their lives. Anxiety could develop into a state where it is hard for a person to maintain a good life. It is through the anxiety that a person will struggle to maintain a sense of peace due to the worries that are persistent.

Anxiety can be treated and resolved if managed by an appropriate plan. Knowing how to control one's sense of anxiety and worry in life can make a difference in what one wishes to do. It is through a general ability to manage anxiety that a person can have more control over one's life and avoid having complicated issues.

Anxiety can be explained:

1. Anxiety occurs where a person develops fears of failing or other problems.

2. The worries that someone has cannot be erased easily.

3. The worries on constantly on the person's mind.

The best way to explain anxiety is that it is like a fear that persists and is hard to control.

What Makes Fear and Anxiety Different?

1. Fear is uneasiness and worries about a very specific thing, whether it is an object, person, or event.

2. Anxiety is more of a general feeling that persists that prevents a person from carrying on normal activities.

For instance, a person might develop anxiety when reading one's phone and noticing there is a symbol stating that someone has an email to read. That person might have anxiety as that person is worried that the email on the phone is from someone that the person is afraid of getting in touch with. This is more pervasive than a basic fear due to the ongoing worries that someone might develop.

Commonplace Worries About Anxious People

Anxiety is a problem that includes several common concerns. These are:

1. An anxious person will feel excessive distress.

It is natural for people to be worried or distressed when they get into situations they are not comfortable with. However, an anxious person will be much more anxious than others. Like with fears, the distress might be very intense and hard to cope with. Unlike fears, those worries could be very dramatic in many instances.

2. Someone might be reluctant to get into certain situations. Sometimes this will go into an outright refusal to do something.

People who are anxious are very suspicious of what they might come across in life. Some people might think about how entering one situation might be dangerous or harmful to them.

3. There might be an ongoing fear of something traumatic happening in a situation.

In the case of anxiety, this is more than just one specific stimulus. This may also involve multiple problems or concerns. The threats involved can be significant and difficult to bear.

4. It might be difficult for a person to get to sleep due to the ongoing worries in one's mind.

Anxiety can cause a person to stop thinking about positive things and instead concentrate on the negatives.

5. An anxious person is not always going to openly declare certain feelings.

Some of the physical symptoms associated with anxiety are important to notice. These include symptoms such as:

- Headaches
- Vomiting and nausea
- A lack of a desire to eat
- Shaking and trembling
- Excessive sweating

Common Anxiety Disorders

There are many types of anxiety disorders a person might experience. These disorders are diverse based on the concerns that people have. Cognitive psychology may help deal with all of these disorders.

Separation Anxiety

Separation anxiety is a condition where a person is worried about what might happen when someone is separated from another person. For instance, a child might be anxious when they are apart from their parents. A married couple could become anxious if they are separated for a period of time. Separation anxiety is more likely to occur in children. Those who have the closest relationships to another will feel the anxiety more severely. Separation anxiety is especially hard for people to resolve. Anxious feelings can last for weeks or months at a time, although it might be easier for a child to get over such a feeling.

Social Anxiety Disorder

Social anxiety disorder is a form of anxiety that impacts a person's ability to talk with other people or to get along with others in a social setting. The most common sign of a social anxiety disorder is when a person is trying to avoid certain situations, especially in public. There are two certain situations to notice:

1. A person might have a generalized fear. This comes across all the social situations someone experiences.

2. A specific fear of a social situation may also occur, such as eating in public, talking to certain people in authority or control, and general public speaking situations.

The fear involved might be based on one's personal performance in a situation. This might include some thoughts that might be dangerous and crippling.

Generalized Anxiety Disorder

A generalized anxiety disorder focuses less on social situations and more about general events. This may be noticed based on how often a person might try to avoid entering into a situation. The challenges that someone enters into while in such a situation can be crippling due to that person feeling a lack of control and support. This problem may be linked up to nausea, diarrhea, or other physical issues that one might develop due to worry. General muscle pains may also develop in some of the worst situations.

The generalized anxiety disorder a person has can come about due to many problems one could enter in. The threats can be dramatic and must be reviewed well to see what can come about in life and how different concerns might develop in general over what one wants to do.

Panic Disorder

A panic disorder is a condition where the feelings of panic will happen at random. This may occur even in cases where the situation seems relatively easy to control. A person with a panic disorder will feel anxiety at various times due to certain triggers. The panic that sets in can cause problems like sweating, a rapid heart rate, dizziness, and even general fears about a situation becoming worse. The damages of such an emotion can be significant and potentially harmful. A panic attack can last for a few minutes or might last for an hour.

Worries About Help or Escape

There might be times where a person is afraid of being in a situation where they might not be able to get help or to escape. This concern is also known as agoraphobia. Several things may be noticed when worrying about one's ability to escape a difficult or troubling situation.

- A person might be afraid of being on public transportation. That person has no control over the vehicle and might not get the help as needed.

- A person could also be afraid of open spaces where it is easy for that person to be targeted. These include parking lots and other spaces where it might be difficult for someone to get the help one needs.

- Enclosed spaces can be just as threatening to some people. These include spaces like shops and theaters. Being in a tight environment with lots of people can be just as threatening.

- Many might also be afraid of what one would do when outside of the house alone.

Selective Mutism

Sometimes a person might be quiet about one's fears or worries. This comes from what is known as selective mutism. Selective mutism is easy to notice. It is a situation where a person is unable to speak in specific situations in life. This comes even though a person was unable to speak in particular situations elsewhere. For instance, a student might feel confident in one's ability to talk to friends in many situations. That person might be vocal in the cafeteria at school or in a parking lot before or after class among other things. But that same student might struggle to speak in other situations. They might not be able to deliver a presentation in class. That someone would freeze up and be unable to think about what to say.

This could be due to a person struggling with situations where they do not have enough information. Maybe it is a situation that is formal. The condition is more common among people who might be new to a certain surrounding. A new student at a school might be more likely to experience selective mutism because they are unaware of what to do to handle a situation in the classroom. A new employee at a workplace might experience selective mutism due to being afraid of what other coworkers might think of them.

Post-Traumatic Stress Disorder

Post-traumatic stress disorder or PTSD is a significant problem for some people. PTSD is a problem where a person experiences anxiety following a traumatic event. PTSD has been associated with people who have served in the military. They might have flashbacks to some of the things that they saw or did while in the field of war. PTSD is a problem that might come about for anyone. A person might develop PTSD as a result of:

- Having accident; this is especially the case for those in auto wrecks

- Victims of assault; this includes people who were subjected to sexual or child abuse

- Suffering a disaster including natural and man-made disasters

- Experiencing a sudden event that caused someone's death or another serious issue

- Struggling with poverty or other financial traumas

The traumas can be significant and often hard to live with. However, it is through those traumas that a person might learn to be stronger and more capable of handling situations in life.

Can a Single Plan Treat Any Kind of Anxiety?

It is true that anxiety can spread quickly in one's mind and might not always be that easy to treat. It is critical for any person who struggles with anxiety to seek treatment. Every person who struggles with anxiety will respond to treatments uniquely and the treatments will vary.

Chapter 25 – Causes of Anxiety

Identifying the issues that cause anxiety is vital to helping people to get over their issues. Cognitive psychology suggests that when the issue is unraveled, it is easier for people to treat the condition.

Social Situations

Social situations can be difficult due to the fact that other people are involved and those people and their actions cannot be controlled. The problems could be dramatic and significant. A person might try to avoid certain social situations with the belief that those events would be dramatic and could add more triggers to one's life than what one can handle at a moment.

Job or School Problems

Anxiety can quickly occur at school or while on the job. For instance, a person might suffer from issues where one has to do something in public or get into a situation where one's work is going to impact other people in some way. A student might have anxiety over being called upon by a teacher. That student might be afraid because they are unsure of what is required of them and they do not know how to communicate with other people in the classroom. For work-related issues, a person might be afraid of what might happen when a manager wants to have a discussion. Nervous feelings could develop because they are fearful or concerned about what might happen in the workplace.

Financial Worries

The financial stresses that someone might feel can surely cause anxiety in anyone's mind. For instance, a person might be afraid of getting into a car wreck because they would be afraid of the monetary issues that will result. Even if one's insurance was to cover everything and they were not going to actually lose money, they still might be anxious about the risk. The fact that the person might lose time at work or hours at school could make the situation problematic because that they may fear what might happen if the injury or other issue caused by the accident were to be serious.

Traumatic Events

Post-traumatic stress disorder or PTSD can be a significant problem that can influence anyone's life depends on how well one's emotions are handled. The depth of anxiety will depend on the severity of the situation that someone might have experienced. People who suffer through traumatic events often try to keep the thoughts surrounding those events private. They might be afraid of what people might think of them if they were open about the situations and the feelings they experience as a result of such events.

Physical Conditions

Genetics could be a factor why someone is likely to develop anxiety. A shortage of oxygen could also be the cause. When a person does not have the oxygen one needs, it becomes harder for that person to act and behave normally. This is not something that will come about every day, and this might only occur in places of high elevation is high.

Chapter 26 – Control Anxiety by Tolerating Uncertainty

Having a plan to manage uncertainty is a part of CBT that assists people to replace the worries they have about unpredictability using some coping mechanisms. More importantly, these mechanisms allow a person to know what to do when experiencing emotional stresses that occur when encountering a difficult situation.

Signs of Intolerance

A great part of anxiety is not being able to handle feelings of uncertainty and not knowing how to cope. Intolerance is an issue where a person is not willing to accept that a certain situation might or might not happen. An intolerant person is not ready to accept that some fear one has could be unwarranted or unlikely.

Some of the things that an intolerant person might do include:

- Find ways to avoid situations

- Delay those situations so as not to have to deal with them

- Look for reassurance to see that one's thoughts or beliefs are fine

- Excessively checking something to see if it is true or false; this may be trying to skew the information to fit someone's personal narrative

- Delay the actions one needs to take to do something

Avoidance Coping

Avoidance coping is a problem that often comes as a result of uncertainty intolerance. This is a situation where a person will try to avoid situations. That person will work very hard to avoid situations that they are unable to predict or control. This form of coping is often a threat that makes life restricted. The main reason a person engages in avoidance coping is that that person feels that something negative might happen. There might be some improper comparisons that the person is making. These include situations where a person assumes that one problem will come about following a certain action. The person will be conditioned to assume that nothing good is going to happen because there are too many things that might go wrong.

Resolving Intolerance

The best thing that a person can do is to be ready to handle the uncertainty in one's life. This can be accomplished by:

1. Determine the specific behaviors one might engage in.

Some of the behaviors that can be analyzed include the following problems:

- seeking reassurance from other people.

- checking something regularly to get an idea of what is happening in a certain situation.

- thinking too long before making a decision. A person is delaying the decision-making process and trying to avoid the consequences.

- procrastinating - waiting until the last minute to do something.

- actively avoiding a situation.

Each of these signs suggests that a person might be struggling to respond and feel comfortable with a situation.

2. Look at the situation that has been presented and think about the possible outcomes.

People who are anxious often assume that very specific outcomes might occur. By considering at all the different outcomes, it becomes easier for someone to get find an answer about dealing with the certain situation.

3. Look at the anxious thoughts and consider how realistic or outlandish some of the thoughts might be.

4. Rank all the problems according to the amount of anxiety that is produced.

Some people might feel worried about responsibilities or tasks or even with everyday routines.

5. Make a list of what can be controlled versus what cannot.

Cognitive psychology suggests that those who understand what they can and cannot do will be more likely to feel at peace. This helps people to make more rational decisions as they understand there are rules as to what they can and cannot do.

6. Become open to accepting certain things that could occur.

The goal is to be more accepting of all the things that might occur in a situation and create a smart plan for handling issues.

7. Write details in a journal details surrounding one's uncertainty.

A separate journal may be used to analyze what someone is doing:

- Include details on what happened when uncertainty was felt and what was done to respond to the concerns at the time.
- One's feelings can also be noted. Was the situation easier to get through than what one thought, or was it a challenge?
- Discuss the things that happened and be as specific as possible.
- List the results of all those events that took place. Talk about what happened and if things went well or did not.
- Review anything that happened in the event that a situation did not turn out the way it was planned. Explain what happened when something wrong happened.

Being able to contextualize the uncertainty in a journal will help to understand how well one is using CBT to manage anxiety.

8. Identify how well one coped with uncertainty.

The person should discuss how well things turned out, particularly if the situation came out just fine and nothing untoward happened. Sometimes the situation at hand will not be significant. In other cases, a person might have got into some trouble and is trying to cope with the outcome. Being able to handle the outcome can be a challenge to manage.

The results of the situation should determine how well a person is able to cope with a situation and if that someone is capable of managing anxiety in even the most negative outcomes or events that might happen in the future. Uncertainty does not have to be a threat in one's life. Working with an open plan and an organized routine is vital to understand that nothing can ever be truly predicted. Being realistic can make an impact on how well someone feels about a situation.

Chapter 27 – Identifying Ruminations

A person who ruminates will think about the negative things that can happen in life and not about the good things that might occur. Ruminations could chain a person down and make it harder for a person to grow and thrive. All those worries can be significant and could make problems worse than they have to be.

What Makes a Rumination Likely To Develop?

Ruminations often take place in the minds of people who are very pessimistic. Those who express naturally pessimistic attitudes will struggle and not know what they can do with their lives. A person may develop ruminations by watching other people as they fail to do things the right way. Someone might see the consequences surrounding an action and will become unhappy with the potential of something similar happening. The threat and worry that might come about in one's life can prove to be a threat that might hurt someone because of the pains and intense fears that someone might hold.

Goal Progress Theory

The goal progress theory of ruminations is when a person is not likely to remember or think about finished tasks. They would instead be fixated on the tasks that were not finished. They think too much about how hard it is to finish. They know that they are not doing much to try and attain certain goals that they wish to reach.

Response Style Theory

Response style theory is another way for ruminations to develop in one's mind. This theory concentrates on being too focused on negative things. Even minute issues that might develop in a situation could become too strong for someone to handle. This does not mean that these problems are going to happen every time, but this could still suggest that a person might not know what to do when encountering a situation.

Types of Ruminations

There are three types of ruminations that may be noticed in a situation. Each concentrates on a certain effect or issue that may develop:

1. State Rumination

A state rumination focuses less on the event and more on the consequences. A person might be worried about failing. The issues that come about following a failure would be the main thing someone is afraid of.

2. Action Rumination

People might think about the actions that they can take to handle some of the goals that they might have. Tasks are analyzed based on the goals and how to correct mistakes.

3. Task-Irrelevant Rumination

People who are not associated with a task may be subjected to task-irrelevant rumination. A person might focus too much on one's surroundings. This includes the setting of an event and the people involved, particularly those who have nothing to do with what is happening. Someone will be too obsessed with what is happening and might concentrate more on the potential for failing and struggling to complete one's tasks correctly.

Thoughts When Ruminating

The thought process that someone goes through during rumination might focus more on some of the problems someone has based on feelings and attitudes that evolve and change over time.

There are three things that a person will think about when ruminating:

1. The feelings about the event in question

These feelings might include something positive or negative. The feelings might be intense, especially if that event involves something very personal.

2. What someone can do to change one's thoughts surrounding that event

There are many ways to change one's attitudes. A person might have different opinions about what someone is doing or thinking at a time.

3. What can be done to keep one's mind from turning to further negative thoughts

Distractions are often helpful, but people are not always going to use them. It might be a challenge to avoid negative thoughts, thus making the rumination a little deeper.

A Process to Identify Ruminations

Ruminations also make it harder for people to make decisions. Several steps can be used to keep ruminations from being a threat:

1. Identify when rumination takes place. This might be when a certain problem grows or becomes somewhat stronger.

2. Look at the accuracy of the rumination.

Most of the ruminations one has might be inaccurate. This happens when people are obsessed with the worst-case scenarios. Those who are too focused on the negative fail to notice the positives.

3. Determine what thoughts cause these ruminations to develop.

The ruminations could be dangerous and harmful. Knowing what causes these ruminations to grow will help people understand the problems that might grow and be harder to live with.

4. Allow thoughts to pass. These include thoughts that make one's life a little harder to handle.

The goal is to let the thoughts, in this case, move through naturally. Those who accept these thoughts and cognitively process them can recognize what they are like and then sort them out based on what is rational versus what is not. Blocking such problems will only make the situation worse and cause a person to become irrational.

Chapter 28 – Cognitive Defusion to Control Anxiety

Anxiety can be controlled by many challenging situations, but one of the most important ones is cognitive defusion. This is a process when a person is removed from one's thoughts. People are often so attached to their thoughts that it becomes next to impossible to resolve worries or fears that might develop.

Cognitive defusion is the opposite of cognitive fusion. In the case of fusion, a person will believe that all of one's thoughts are accurate and true. Cognitive defusion is where a person will acknowledge thoughts as basic thoughts. That is, they are not necessarily thoughts that are always true – they are just thoughts that come along as they are. There is no need to believe or disbelieve any of them. Cognitive defusion can work for any negative thoughts that one has.

When Does Cognitive Defusion Work?

Cognitive defusion is a part of cognitive therapy that may work in situations like the following:

- When someone is feeling negative about the thoughts that they are having and where the thoughts are too depressing or are making one's work harder to manage.

- Someone who has a low self-worth could use cognitive defusion to reorganize their thoughts and treat them differently.

- People who worry too much and need to remove the emotions to keep worries from being too intense.

- Those who suffer from OCD-related anxiety or fears can benefit as defusion reduces the intensity of compulsive thoughts.

- Those who might be living in the past and are playing the same memories or thoughts several times over need cognitive defusion to lessen the intensity of those thoughts.

How to Use Cognitive Defusion

The following steps can be used to keep the problems of difficult thoughts from being more of a burden than necessary:

1. Acknowledge the thought.

Be thankful for the thought no matter what it might be. Interpreting the meaning of the thought helps to create a sense of clarity. At this point, it becomes easy to let go of the memory after a period of time. The thought does not have to be acknowledged for too long. Sometimes just looking at the thought for a few seconds is good enough.

2. Change the focus.

Do not continue focusing on a certain issue. It helps to go into another room or area or maybe even change whatever action someone is doing. This keeps the original thought that came about from being too intense. Pay attention to something different without necessarily passing judgment on the thought that just occurred. The focus does not have to be on something relating to the same topic either. The new topic can be radically removed from what one was thinking about earlier. The only need is to change the feelings and thoughts one has before they can become harder to deal with.

3. Observe the issue.

After the focus is changed, the intensity of the thought is slightly weakened. An observation like "I am thinking about ……." is often good enough. This is enough to acknowledge the presence without the thought becoming intense and the feelings of anxiety need to be curbed.

4. Be aware of the judgmental words that are being used as the thought occurs.

Sometimes a person might assume that something is either "good" or "bad." It is best to use more descriptive words that might be more honest or generous in nature. Saying that a thought was "helpful" or "unhelpful" might be a better choice.

5. Get back to the present.

After looking at the situation, return to the present and think about what is going on right now. Avoid looking back into the past and replace the thoughts with something more productive or efficient. The issues that someone has should be defused at this point. The difficult problems one has can be kept from being pervasive or otherwise likely to thrive or grow. The best part of the process is that it only takes a few seconds for this to work.

Preparation

While the process of cognitive defusion can work, it is even better when the right preparations are considered. The following efforts for preparation may be used to keep the situation under control:

- Determine the situations in which negative thoughts are likely to take place. Consider possible replacement thoughts with regards to a situation.

- Review the realistic nature of the situations.

- Look at the situations one might encounter. Is there some kind of trigger point or other feature in a situation that might make it easier for someone to do more? This works only in cases where someone knows what to do when keeping a thought realistic.

Planning for cognitive defusion is needed for getting more out of one's work. Knowing how to manage certain thoughts the right way and how to keep those worries from being a burden should help anyone to grow and succeed.

Chapter 29 – Recognizing Intrusive Memories

Many of the memories someone will have related to the events that took place in their lives. These events, as mentioned earlier, are episodic memories. They can be detailed, and they are often autobiographical in nature. Those memories are usually positive and can be recalled as pleasant. Some of the memories people might experience include those that are difficult and in some cases make the anxiety one feels worse. These memories are called intrusive memories.

For instance, Jeff might have memories relating to his days in high school. He might recall moments when he felt happy to be with his friends and learned some great things from many professors who were positive and happy to help. However, Jeff might recall an event that was not pleasant such as a car accident while driving to school. Perhaps he has a memory of trying to give a presentation but failing because he was too nervous.

Those negative memories will cause him to feel anxiety. He might begin to worry once again about not doing well in a social situation or maybe getting into another accident in his car. In this situation, Jeff had some intrusive memories that got in the way of the good ones. These were hidden in his mind for a while. He might not have been aware that he had those memories until they surfaced.

Characteristics of Intrusive Memories

Intrusive memories can be about anything that might have happened in one's life. There are some types of intrusive memories that might be more prominent than others. Here are a few of the general characteristics of intrusive memories.

1. Intrusive memories are triggered without warning.

When a person thinks of something, an intrusive memory will almost surely happen and trigger one's anxiety further.

2. The memory returns automatically.

When a memory like this happens, it becomes easy for someone to be worried or confused. The intrusive memory will develop due to a person having a memory that links directly to the old one. In Jeff's case, the memory of a car accident returned as he was thinking about hanging out with his friends. The relationship of his high school days to that particular event is very close.

3. The intrusive memory can be vivid.

Many intrusive memories can be intense and more detailed than others. Part of this is due to the negative imagery and feelings that the memory produced.

For Jeff, the imagery that comes with the car accident could be vivid. He might recall the sound of his car getting hit or the panic he felt afterward when he wasn't sure if he was hurt. The worries that he had were intense and they left an impact on him. The vivid nature of his memory makes it feel as though he is reliving that moment in time.

4. The memory could be about any event, but in most cases, it involves a traumatic event.

One of the greatest problems with life is that the positive memories are always fleeting, and yet the negative memories will persist. Those memories are ones that cause a person to feel a sense of panic and dread. A person who has regular anxiety issues might suffer from regular flashbacks. This is especially the case for those who have PTSD and cannot stop reliving certain traumatic events in their lives. When a flashback occurs, someone will have a feeling that the trauma that one experienced returns in a vivid form. All the pressure and stress that one experienced will return. The mental and emotional anxiety and feelings that occurred at the time will return and disrupt all other feelings and make concentration difficult.

Addressing Memories

The best strategy in cognitive psychology to handle harmful memories is to acknowledge their presence and to let them move off to the wayside. The memories should only be recognized for a few seconds. Dwelling upon those memories for too long only makes it harder for the mind to focus and concentrate on what someone wishes to do.

A few steps can be used to handle one's memory and to make it a little easier to identify and review:

1. Notice when the memory in question happens.

The memory might come about at random.

2. Notice how that memory relates to the first memory that triggered it.

The memory that was produced can be compared with the original memory someone had.

3. Find a way to reserve one's focus on the main memory one is trying to utilize.

There should be some trigger that makes it easier for the original memory to be recalled.

4. Decide if the negative memory can be contextualized.

Some sense of context might be noticed in a memory, but in most cases, the memory will just be something triggered due to some sensory data or some connection that comes with an outside stimulus. Being aware of how those memories are developed will keep the problem from being worse.

Chapter 30 – How To Become Mindful to Ease Anxiety

Mindfulness is a special part of managing anxiety that deserves to be discussed in detail. Mindfulness is often incorporated into cognitive therapy processes as a means of getting away from negative thought patterns including those that can cause a person to develop anxiety and struggle to manage the situation. Mindfulness is a practice that focuses on helping a person to relax and be at ease with the self. The effort involves physical efforts to keep calm and positive and give someone the power needed to keep one's mind from being overburdened by difficult problems that may develop.

A person who is mindful will have an easier time handling one's feelings and worries. Keeping those problems in control makes it easier for someone to feel positive and relaxed with what one wants to do.

There are several positive things that come from being mindful:

- The ruminations that someone has will become less frequent or pervasive. This reduces the risk for negative thoughts to occur or for one to focus too much on the same things or issues.

- It becomes easier for people to not avoid issues or other problems when they are mindful and ready to handle the subject matter.

- People can also make better and smarter choices when the right plans for handling life are managed.

Mindfulness is a necessity for people to follow when finding a way to become happier and in control.

The steps for being mindful are:

    1. Think about what is happening in one's mind.

Knowing how to manage certain problems that might develop and to keep them from being so strong is vital to one's success. Sensory information should be reviewed alongside points on how easy it is for tasks to be finished.

    2. Relax for a few minutes each day.

Take time to relax for a bit of time each day. People can do anything they want to relax. The key is to keep from being overly stimulated.

- Practice meditation to relax. Meditation helps people to focus their thoughts on certain things and to learn how to concentrate.

- Perform aromatherapy - oils in a diffuser in one's room. The relaxing scents might help to clear one's thoughts.

- Go to a quiet room and think about what has gone on throughout the day. Consider how certain events occurred through the actions that took place in the day.

- Take deep and calming breaths regularly. Keeping one's breath in check makes it easier for someone to feel rested and relaxed.

Any of these practices can work in any situation.

    3. Recognize certain feelings as they occur.

Consider some of the feelings that were produced during the day and what caused those feelings to come about. How did they go away? These points should be explored to figure out what causes those feelings to grow and become intense in some situations.

4. Have more breaks during the day.

It is understandable why people might try to do as much work as they can. People might work ten or twelve or even fifteen hours a day at times. They might do so because they feel they need more money or they are afraid of letting people down by saying no to certain tasks. All that work can become problematic. It becomes easier for a person to become stressed. This causes a person to feel anxious and worried. Adding breaks during the day helps a person feel more comfortable with one's work. Those who relax and take breaks regularly will not be likely to make errors while on the job.

5. Always acknowledge the progress one makes.

Being able to recognize the progress to complete a task is vital for success. This gives a clear idea of what someone is doing and how well the efforts one has put in are working.

6. Be kind about any criticism.

Sometimes criticism is warranted. Cognitive psychology suggests that those who link faults and other issues to positive thoughts will have an easier time moving forward in life. Therefore, it helps to be positive about any faults that one has. The happiest people who feel no anxiety are those who accept themselves for who they are and are not afraid to accept criticism. Criticisms help people to find new things that they can do to grow their lives and feel stronger about who they are. Each of these steps for mindfulness will go a long way toward handling one's anxiety. Mindfulness is an aspect of cognitive psychology that lets people link what they are thinking to their actions, thus making their work more valuable.

Exercise Ideas for Mindfulness

Several exercises can be used to help people become mindful and in control. The goal of these exercises is to think about something that causes anxiety or another negative feeling and to let that problem go by the wayside. Getting rid of the burden that comes along is needed for preventing significant problems get worse and otherwise be a challenge.

1. In the mind, spray paint a thought onto a vehicle like a train car or van. Watch that vehicle move down the road or railway to watch it disappear. This exercise lets a person notice some of the worries or emotional problems disappear.

2. Watch a thought as it appears on a billboard on the road. Imagine driving past that billboard or going through a tunnel that keeps the billboard from being visible.

3. Watch as the clouds form in the sky and see how they disappear after a while. Imagine one's thoughts as those clouds. Look as they appear and eventually disappear.

4. Look how a stream flows along and the water moves by. See any natural items that might be flowing along with the water. These might represent the thoughts one has. These can flow by and keep one's mind from having the same thoughts all the time.

Just knowing how to visualize these thoughts as they move away and stop bothering one's mind is often good enough for keeping issues from being too pervasive.

How Long Does Mindfulness Take?

Mindfulness is a practice that requires a bit of training. People can spend as much time as they want to manage their emotions and to use mindfulness to make one's train of thought easier to handle. Expect to spend a bit of extra time with trying to handle one's feelings of mindfulness to calm anxiety. After the issue disappears, it should become a little easier for problems to be resolved.

The Physical Effects of Mindfulness

Mindfulness should help a person rest and feel relaxed. The body will still feel alert regarding other things. The mindful feelings that someone develops could help to relax the mind and therefore keep the body from having an increase in blood pressure rate or heart rate. It is through the amygdala that the body is capable of handling the stresses or worries that one has.

Can Mindfulness Occur Right After a Triggering Situation?

Those who have triggering events in their lives might feel as though they cannot do more for themselves because the emotional and mental pressures they are in are too strong. Mindfulness-related practices can be used at any time of day and in any place. Remember that mindfulness is designed to work to keep the thoughts one has and the feelings or issues under control. More importantly, this helps to prevent certain problems relating to one's thoughts from being pervasive and difficult.

Chapter 31 – Progressive Muscle Relaxation

Another part of cognitive behavioral therapy that relates to being mindful involves the use of progressive muscle relaxation. Knowing how to manage one's muscles and to keep them from feeling stressed is vital for one's success. As a person becomes anxious or fearful, the muscles start to become tense. Progressive muscle relaxation helps to keep those physical stresses under control. The main purpose of PMR is to rest the muscles in two key steps. First, specific muscles will be targeted. All the tension that was produced from the anxiety or another worry can be released.

PMR helps people reduce the effects of headaches, stomachaches, and the ongoing desire to dwell on a negative thought. As the stresses are removed, the mind will be more productive and emotionally organized. There is also a potential for the body to get to sleep quicker when the muscles are relaxed. Progressive muscle relaxation is great for managing the physical issues of anxiety. PMR helps people establish cues for what they can do when they have worrying feelings that trigger anxiety.

It is easier to feel confident and comfortable when the body is relaxed and refreshed. The brain will notice when the body starts to get tense, thus helping a person to come up with a plan for resolving the issue via PMR.

The Steps

This practice of PMR requires some preparation at the start.

1. Find a quiet and calm place to practice this for at least 15 minutes.

2. Add a small bit of tension into the body at the beginning.

Consider the target muscle that is feeling tense. Add a small amount of tension to that area. For instance, some tension can be applied onto one's shoulders by having the hands grab onto the shoulders and squeeze lightly. Do this for about five seconds to allow the muscles to feel the added pressure.

3. Wait for a few seconds and then release the tension that was added to the muscle.

Exhale and let out all the tension that was produced. Focus on how the tension disappears. Recognize the release.

4. Stay in a relaxed state for a few moments. It only takes about 15 seconds for the body to feel rested. Do not try to rush the process. Focus on the tension as it is released.

5. Move on to the next part of the body that might be experiencing stress.

Allow the stresses to be released without adding lots of pressure. Be cautious and careful when doing this so it becomes easier for the body to release all the stresses.

6. While this takes place, visualize something positive while relieving one's tensions.

Whatever is being visualized can be used to help keep the mind from feeling lots of pressure or worry. The new image is linked to the process can be brought up in one's mind while relaxing. As the positive image comes up in one's mind, it becomes easier for the pressure one has to be released. This exercise can be done a few times in a day if needed. Getting enough practice helps anyone to train so that managing PMR becomes second nature after a while. This practice can be used even when someone is not actually feeling any anxiety. It might be better to practice this when one is not feeling anxious as it gives a control period for someone to try this out.

How is the Body Targeted?

This muscle relaxation process works best when the body is targeted in this order:

1. Foot and leg area; these areas can be massaged

2. The stomach and chest; further massaging is needed

3. Hand and arm area; stretch these parts of the body outward

4. Neck and shoulders; a mix of both stretching and massaging

5. Various areas around the head; opening one's mouth wide, clenching the eyelids shut, and raising one's eyebrows up high along the forehead

The lower parts of the body are to be targeted first as this is believed to be where the energy starts. Some argue that the feet are the key parts of the body that can benefit the most from relaxation therapy. As the process of relaxation continues, it should become a little easier for people to feel comfortable and in check with their bodies.

Chapter 32 – The Art of Positive Criticism

No one likes a critic, but it is through criticism that people learn what they are doing right versus what is wrong. But it is through the worst criticism that it becomes harder for a person to live and feel better about whatever it is one may wish to do at a moment.

One of the main reasons why people become so anxious is because they are overly critical of themselves. They think that all the things they are doing are wrong. They will judge themselves based on all the bad things they have got into and how hard it is for them to get over those problems. The hostile feelings they have toward themselves will make their lives harder to manage and can cause strong judgmental feelings. The hassles involved in this case could prove to be too dramatic for some due to the harsh thoughts that come along.

It is true that many people think about the negative things in their lives when it comes to criticism. People are more likely to cognitively think about the negative stuff that comes along above all other things. Those who focus on all the negative points might become equally negative themselves because of all those people they have entered into.

The criticism could become far too much for some people if it is too intense or pervasive. The immense amount of criticism one might enter into can be tough to live with and might cause a person to feel judged far too much. The excessive judgment and criticism that one is subjected will cause a problem in one's life. This all happens without creating any comfortable feelings in the process.

Fortunately, there is a form of criticism that may be utilized to improve upon one's ability to manage anxiety and to start thinking more positive things. This art is known as positive criticism. Positive criticism is an act where a person concentrates on the positive aspects of something that people often ignore. The key is to look at something that might make a person happy or confident in whatever is happening at a time.

How Positive and Constructive Criticism Differ

Positive criticism is similar to constructive criticism in that they both focus on ways to make things better. However, there is a massive difference between the two. In constructive criticism, a person will be made to consider how negatives can be changed into positives. Although this form of criticism might be valuable to some, it is also a practice that is not always easy for all people to accept.

Positive criticism concentrates on the good things about a situation. With a positive approach, a person will start to notice all the great things that are happening in one's routines and attitudes. This creates a better approach to life. By focusing on the positive things, a person will start to notice what someone is doing correctly. This includes all the great outcomes of one's actions and how well certain behaviors might be working in one's favor.

Using Positive Criticism

The things that can be done to handle positive criticism are simple:

1. Start by focusing more on the situation at hand. It is the situation involved that makes the greatest impact of all.

The situation that someone might be anxious about should be analyzed based on the good things that might happen on that occasion.

2. Consider some of the alternatives that can be used in a situation.

The goal to find alternatives is not to think about the possible negative outcomes, but to find and concentrate on the possible positive outcomes.

3. Consider how realistic the positive criticism is.

The most important thing to do when finding a way to stay positive is to be realistic. Trying too hard to be positive might make the criticism sound artificial in nature. More importantly, being realistic ensures that the positive criticism is sincere. It is through realism that it becomes easier for people to feel appreciated and supported. Positive criticism helps people recognize what they are doing and the positive outcomes. The most important point is that a person will feel less anxiety as the brain starts to consider some of the positives of a situation. This, in turn, produces an optimistic feeling that provides a sense of encouragement and interest in a task.

Chapter 33 – Addressing Anxiety Head-On Through Rational Emotive Behavior Therapy

Anxiety often happens because a person does not feel comfortable. It is up to that someone to get in direct contact with the issues through rational emotive behavior therapy. This is a practice that concentrates on how well a person can manage one's emotions and thoughts. The goal of rational emotive behavior therapy is to look at many of the issues that someone might feel or experience when getting in touch with something one is anxious about. This is similar to what someone might do when trying to manage fears. While the fear tree and other similar ideas focus on gradual exposure, the rational emotive behavior therapy, or REBT, focuses on jumping right in to get the answers one needs to resolve a fear and prevent the issues from becoming worse.

Background of REBT

To understand why REBT is so valuable, it helps to look at how the process was first developed and how it was planned. The practice was devised by Albert Ellis, a psychologist who developed an interesting process that would allow him to talk with many women. He found that his fear of talking to women would start to disappear when he started to talk to more women at a time. This led Ellis to develop the REBT process. He noticed that the best way to manage one's emotions is by controlling the negative thought patterns. His belief was that people are not turned off by certain things. Rather, they are turned off due to their views of certain things.

In the case of his experience with women, Ellis found that he did not hate women in the least. Rather, he had negative thoughts about how they would respond to him while also not respecting him. Through the regular exposure that Ellis had toward many women, it became clear to him that his negative impressions about how he could work alongside women would help him to feel more confident among those women.

Ellis used a three-point process in the REBT system:

1. There is going to be an activating event that someone encounters locally.

2. A belief will be linked to that event. This belief might be a certain feeling about whatever is going on at the moment.

3. The emotional response that comes from a belief must be listed next. This is the consequence of the belief.

All beliefs are linked to certain emotions and feelings. By working alongside those sudden beliefs or attitudes, one can understand why they think certain ways and recognize the links that they have to certain ideas.

Managing the Routine

The process that Ellis developed will help people to notice what they can do to control their emotions and to keep them under control in any circumstance.

1. Start by taking a look at an irrational thought.

The first part of the process is to think about the certain irrational thought that was developed in one's mind and how it might have been harbored. Knowing how that thought developed and what caused that thought to grow helps a person to recognize the issues that one might have. Some of the most common irrational thoughts that Ellis targeted when he devised REBT were feelings about how others behave or personalization. These cognitive distortions were seen by Ellis as problems that make it harder for people to process information correctly and to feel comfortable about what they encounter.

The irrational thoughts that are produced are often interpreted as beliefs or absolutes that must be true. Although they are not accurate in the least, they can become a problem.

2. Find challenges to those illogical thoughts.

To make this work, the REBT process must entail a logical approach to handling these thoughts. Many of the processes listed in this guide are about being kind and finding one's way around issues. With REBT, a person must analyze the illogical issues one has and how those problems might have been developed. Confronting illogical thoughts and ideas bluntly might sound rough to some, but it allows a person to manage certain processes and emotional functions.

3. Look at what is causing the thought to be illogical.

There has to be some reason why an idea is considered illogical. The problem must be explored and mentally analyzed.

4. Determine the effects of having that irrational thought.

Understanding the damage being caused by the irrational thought is crucial to one's overall success.

5. After recognizing the impact of that illogical thought, a new solution can be produced. A rational alternative action or idea can be planted in one's mind.

The best thing to do in this case is to replace the problematic concern in one's mind with something more sensible. REBT is a fascinating aspect of CBT that is not hard to understand and can help anyone to go far with a certain plan for using the right and most logical thoughts possible.

Chapter 34 – Understanding Depression

Depression is one of the most misunderstood mental disorders. This is a problem that can be serious and can lead to self-harm and isolation. Depression has been closely linked to suicidal thoughts or actions. To outsiders, depression appears to be a condition where someone just feels sad and tired most of the time. To those who suffer from depression, it is where negative feelings become pervasive to the point where it is next to impossible for a person to do the things one wants to do in life.

Cognitive behavioral therapy may work to help control depression and to help a person feel more positive about life. This would require an immense amount of support and assistance because depression is hard to figure out and control. When managed appropriately, the risk of harmful behaviors as a result of one's depression can be potentially reduced. The difficult feelings that someone has a need to be challenged to ensure a person will not suffer from dramatic problems relating to depression.

What Causes Depression?

Depression is a problem that involves a person feeling hopeless or unhappy for an extensive amount of time. The situation causes a person to feel as though nothing good is going to happen and nothing is going to change that. The emotional burden is a problem, but it is also a condition that many people are not fully aware of. Many do not understand what causes depression.

Genetics

Genetics may cause depression to develop in some people. Those who have family members who suffered from depression are more likely to experience depression themselves. It is not fully clear as to why genetics play such a role in depression. Just look online to find various studies surrounding genetics and depression.

Impacts In the Brain

The brain could be a factor as to why depression might develop in one's mind. The neurotransmitters in one's brain might become unbalanced. This is especially the case with dopamine, a transmitter that regulates feelings of happiness.

This often leads to people using medications to control feelings of depression. Although some medications are used to temporarily resolve depressed feelings, they are not necessarily going to treat the deeper cause of the depression.

Hormonal Changes

As the body's hormones change, it becomes harder for a person to manage one's emotions. The emotional impact of hormonal changes makes it harder for a person to have healthy emotions. This, in turn, keeps the mind from being in control.

Women are often more likely to develop depression as a result of hormonal changes. The impacts of such changes during menopause can be dramatic and often hard for many women to adjust.

Seasonal Affective Disorder

Seasonal affective disorder, or SAD, is a condition where a person experiences a disturbance in sleeping habits. This often occurs during the winter season when the days are shorter and hours of daylight are less. This change in light impacts the natural rhythms of the body. A person can experience sudden and persistent fatigue. Although SAD is not something that all people will experience, it is a threat to some. The problems that occur due to SAD can be dramatic and hard for some people to live through because they are unavoidable and often entail regular routines being dramatically disrupted. SAD may also be made worse by a person is being in touch with one's friends as often and the winter can be isolating. People who live in colder climates where the days are shorter are typically more likely to suffer from SAD-related problems.

Stresses in Life

Sometimes the immense stresses that people might experience can become too hard for them to live with. Those stresses can make life difficult. It is widely believed that the hormonal changes that occur during high-stress situations might be a factor in what causes a person to change attitudes or behaviors. Cortisol is produced when the body feels stress. This hormone can influence how serotonin, dopamine, and other hormones are produced. The imbalance in brain chemicals can cause a person's natural brain functions to stop working accordingly. This, in turn, increases the likelihood for someone to develop depression.

Moments of Grief

Intense feelings of grief that someone might experience can become serious and significant, such as grief from traumatic events and especially from the loss of a loved one. The lack of a desire to do normal tasks following a significant loss will only make one's life harder. The specific causes of one's depression will vary for each person. Understanding what may cause someone to experience depression may help with determining what can be done to help that person.

The Depression Cycle

To fully understand what makes depression hard to live with, it is important to look at how the depression cycle works.

1. In the beginning, a person will suffer from a lack of energy.

The lack of energy does not have to just be physical fatigue. It could be struggling to have interest or enthusiasm. For instance, a person might be bored with the same job or routine of every day. That someone will start to lose interest in something because everything is just the same each day.

2. The beginnings of neglect.

A depressed person will start to do fewer things and will stop following regular routines are accepting normal responsibilities.

3. The guilt will increase.

Because of the neglect and lack of interest, it becomes easier for someone to feel guilty and unhappy with one's life. They will feel hopeless and ineffective in life due to how one is unable to complete certain jobs or take part in regular activities.

4. The human mind will feel tired and positive thoughts will be elusive.

The lack of work and activity the inability will lead to intense depression. The problem will get worse as it continues.

5. The cycle will start all over again. Those negative feelings will lead to a further loss of interest.

The worst part of the cycle of depression is that it will continue and become more severe the longer the cycle persists.

Common Effects to Watch For

To treat someone who is suffering from depression, it is vital to look at the effects of the depression. These problems are among the more common concerns to watch for:

1. A person's mood might change.

A person might be struggling to stay interested in some of the things that a person would normally be interested in. Someone might say that one's mood is sad. That someone is not satisfied with what is happening.

2. A person might not have the same interest that one had.

The interest that someone has in something can be measured based on how much enthusiasm a person shows in wanting to do something. A depressed person might lose all that interest. Maybe someone who was interested in going to a certain event every week might have stopped going to that event altogether.

3. There might be noticeable changes in one's weight.

People who are depressed are likely to either gain or lose weight. This includes a weight that a person is not intentionally trying to lose or gain. A person might gain weight from eating to feel better. Someone might lose weight due to a lack of interest in food.

4. Someone might experience dramatic changes in sleeping habits.

Some of the more common changes in sleep are either sleeping too much or not getting to sleep at all. A person might feel tired even after waking up or tired at various points throughout the day.

5. There could be a lack of the ability to concentrate.

Those who are frequently depressed might not know how to concentrate or make decisions because they lack the interest to stay involved.

6. The worst situations are people who might regularly think about death or self-harm.

It is natural for people to be afraid of death, but a depressed person will have a greater focus on the possibility of death. The added preoccupation that someone has toward death could be a sign that someone is willing to cause themselves harm.

What Are the Long-Term Effects?

The worst part about depression is that it can become extremely serious if the concern is not managed appropriately. Depression can be devastating as the issue makes someone feel worried or panicked about life. Depression makes it harder for a person to do anything. It keeps people from feeling comfortable around others. Relationships and friendships can be hurt because a person might be isolating themselves from others. Depression is a mental concern that may lead people into harming themselves. The worst cases often include suicidal thoughts or actions because a person might feel unhappy with one's life while feeling that it is not going to get any better.

Men or Women?

Women are often more likely to experience depression than men. The main reason for this is how they respond to depressing events or other things that are too hard. A man is likely to distract himself when he comes across a problem in his life. He might struggle to deflect his attention from a problem, thus making it easier for him to be judgmental and hard on himself. A woman would be more likely to ruminate about what she is experiencing. She will think about the problems and how it is keeping her from feeling happy. That burden will make it harder for her to concentrate and enjoy activities. This does not mean that men are not likely to ruminate about things, nor does it mean women are not going to try to distract themselves from the issues they encounter.

Can Depression Be Cured?

Depression is often seen as a lifelong issue that will change things in one's life and make it harder for a person to think and carry on normally. Depression makes it hard for people to live healthy lives and to think straight all the time. It is through the work provided by CBT that the effects of depression and the emotional worries that are produced by this condition can be resolved. Depression is a very dramatic problem that must be controlled. Cognitive psychological ideas might help in resolving the situation.

Chapter 35 – Dialectal Behavior Therapy

One of the best solutions for managing depression with CBT is through dialectal behavior therapy or DBT. Originally designed as a practice to help people with borderline personality disorder, dialectal behavior therapy has become an essential part of managing depression. The purpose of dialectal behavior therapy is to teach new skills to people who might experience dramatic emotional or mental issues. People can use the new skills to regulate their emotions and to tolerate uncertainty or worries that might be unavoidable.

Reversing the Depression Cycle

The goal of dialectal behavior therapy is to assist in reversing the depression cycle that one experiences. In short:

1. A person will feel more energy.

2. The activities that a person engages in will become more proficient.

3. The person becomes more hopeful and active while not feeling guilty.

4. The depression that one had will start to dissipate.

5. The cycle perpetually repeats itself.

The Many Parts of DBT

There are several aspects of dialectal behavior therapy that can be used to control the impact of depression on one's life.

1. The experience of depression should be discussed.

The behaviors that someone exhibits should be explored. This includes a review of the types of behaviors that one has versus the efforts one might regularly use to control them. A person has to understand how one's depression evolves and the problems that develop.

2. The patient's most dangerous behaviors must be treated.

Any attempts at harm or suicide among other serious threats should be addressed at the start. CBT focuses on what can be done to correct serious emotional problems. This is not a stage that will work in all cases as some people with depression have not tried to hurt themselves, but it is a part of the process that has to be used to keep a person from being at risk of further harm.

3. After those issues are covered, a person can discuss one's tolerance for certain emotional problems.

The person's emotions should be analyzed based on how intense they are and whether or not a person is capable of handling those emotions properly. A person has to look at those emotions based on how often they occur and how intense they are.

4. The emotions that are being felt must be realized and labeled.

Being able to recognize the emotions one holds will help to make DBT issues from being difficult. The quick identification of these emotions helps to give someone an idea of what is causing depression to develop.

5. After the emotions are identified, they can be controlled through new visualization or imagery-based functions.

The visualizations might be varied, but it is up to an individual to figure out what can be done to resolve a certain problem.

6. New strategies to organize thoughts must be included.

The strategies used for managing thoughts can include one of the many that were covered earlier in this guide. The goal is to replace negative stimuli with positive ones or to rethink the validity or logistics of the thoughts one has. Looking into the issues one holds and considering the alternatives or ways to explain those concerns helps to organize one's thoughts and reducing the risk of significant harm resulting.

7. A focus is placed on both self-esteem and improved relationships with other people.

Self-esteem is often missing among many people who have depression. The key for managing thoughts is to organize one's emotions and feelings around other people. The key is to look at the situations that can cause a person's self-esteem to improve. The situations involved might be events that promote pleasure or allow a person to be near others easily. Being capable of recognizing all the things in one's life that produce happiness is vital to have a better chance to feel confident and comfortable with the things one might wish to do in life in general.

Chapter 36 – Scheduling Pleasant Events

Everyone loves to take part in fun events. It is through these events that people can feel happy and excited. For such events to be worthwhile, it is critical for people to focus on taking part in pleasant events that are enjoyable. People who engage in pleasant activities that they can enjoy will feel more confident in themselves and less likely to experience depression. Scheduling great events to enjoy throughout one's life helps to find joy every day.

Behaviors that people can use to manage the depression cycle:

1. Activities can be scheduled to help someone feel better.
2. Activities can also keep a person from feeling tired.
3. These events may also help a person to think clearly.

Why Does This Work for CBT?

Scheduling pleasant events for CBT purposes might seem like a basic idea. After all, anyone can plan certain events in a day. It is through the special events one arranges that life can be a little more enjoyable and worth living. It is through pleasant events that people can replace the thoughts of dread and unhappiness in their lives with something to look forward to.

What Types of Events Can Work?

The events that can be scheduled can include anything so long as it is healthy. Many things can work at a time:

- A person can call a friend. This could include talking with that person about what is happening in one's life and what things of interest are developing.

- Going to a sporting event or a movie with a friend or two.

- Traveling might be fun to do. This could include something that is not too far from one's home but could be something that is entertaining.

Anything that is out of the ordinary could be planned. A person does not necessarily have to plan something elaborate. All it takes is just something that is fun and worth doing. Just doing something new can make a difference in how a person feels. The person who plans these events should think about what makes those events worthwhile and interesting.

Discovering New Skills

One idea to manage depression is to find new skills in life. People who discover new skills are more likely to feel as though they can do anything. For instance, a person might learn how to ride a motorcycle or how to cook Italian food. Whatever it might be, a person who discovers new skills and capabilities makes it easier to feel happy with what one can do in life. The new skills that one discovers should help improve one's mind and replace the difficult thoughts one has with new ones that give a feeling of pleasure.

Finding new skills is great with CBT needs in mind for many reasons:

- New skills help a person to develop a sense of self-worth.

- New skills will help people feel confident about other skills or attitudes that they might have.

- It is easier to create positive connections with others if someone can show a sense of interest in some way.

Remember that any kind of skill of interest to one can be utilized. People should find a way to have more fun and feel confident about one's life.

Managing Activities

People have to do more than just schedule fun activities to look forward to. They also have to list information on how they are capable of experiencing. The following steps should work to manage one's emotions with regards to these events.

1. Plan an event to take place at a certain time and day.

2. List specific information on the activity that will take place in a guidebook.

3. Enter in details on how intense one's depression feels before the event. This can be listed on a scale from 0 to 10.

4. After the event takes place, write down detailed information on what happened during the event.

5. Enter in a number indicating how strong one's depression was after the event. Again, this is from a scale of 0 to 10.

6. Repeat this with many other events in the future.

It always helps to have something positive to do every day or at least every other day. Decide what activities might be more attractive or at least effective in countering one's feelings of depression.

7. Review many of these events after a few weeks of keeping the journal. Look at which events appear to have produced the best results in countering one's depression.

The events that were rated as being the best in controlling feelings of depression can help determine the specific stimuli or ideas to reduce the impact of one's depression. More importantly, this looks at the things that can be done to produce the best possible effects. Managing these effects makes it easier for people to know how to control their thoughts. By knowing what is more effective in controlling one's emotions, it becomes easier for a person to feel happy and positive over the things that someone wants to do in life. Replacing negative behaviors with more positive ones could make a difference in understanding what can be used to make life stronger and more comfortable.

What About Responsibilities?

Responsibilities can be complicated and in some cases could be ones that a person has neglected because of depression. Such responsibilities might involve doing things with family members, managing critical tasks at one's place of work, or simply handling random tasks around the house. People with depression have the option to plan these responsibilities and choose to list information on the tasks that will provide a sense of relief or satisfaction after they are finished. People who do not complete their daily responsibilities will feel overwhelmed and stressed. Life will seem worse when the duties that one has started to pile up and become too hard to manage.

Of course, plenty of rest should be planned as well. A person needs the right amount of rest to have extra time to complete tasks. Planning the best possible events is always helpful when looking at CBT practices. By working with such events, a person can reverse the cycle of depression.

Chapter 37 – Successive Approximation to Manage Depression

One reason people often become depressed is that they have so many tasks to complete in their lives that it becomes a huge burden for them to handle. It only takes a few minutes for a couple of tasks to add up and become a huge burden that can prove to be a difficult concern to live with. Successive approximation is a psychological construct that cognitively encourages the mind to control how certain tasks are to be completed.

The Basic Approach

The general approach of successive approximation is that it helps people to tackle certain tasks or routines by taking larger jobs and breaking them down into a series of smaller ones. The goal of successive approximation is to make depression less prevalent by helping a person to feel confident in what one can do in life. The human mind might receive a seed of an idea suggesting that one cannot do certain things because they have to complete tasks that include an unrealistic number of steps. People who are subjected to things that they cannot realistically do or feel they cannot complete will experience depression.

Successive approximation reduces the stresses that one has and gives a person a more controlled plan of what one wants to do. Those who concentrate on something simpler and easier to manage will be capable of managing their thoughts better. More importantly, the negative thoughts that someone has cognitively added into one's mind will be reduced in intensity. This, in turn, adds a better approach for managing work. Such a task is especially critical when it comes to managing depression. This mental issue is significant and can take a while for a person to get over, if at all. By working with this strategy, it becomes easier for someone to progressively manage the worries and issues that they might have.

Good to Handle Fears

Successive approximation can be used by those who have intense fears as well. Many people have strong fears of many situations that they feel are too overwhelming. These include fears of issues or situations where a person might be told to work a little harder than necessary. The challenge associated with complicated events can be reduced by successive approximation.

Prepare Sub-goals

The first part of successive approximation is to look at the sub-goals of a complete task. Part of this includes looking at the extensive task at hand and what can be done to get through the entire process. Break an entire task into many mini-tasks. An example of this is Kim as she tries to get the courage to finally take her driver's license test. She might have been waiting for a long time to take her test, and she is feeling depressed about it because she knows she needs a car if she wants to go places and do more things with other people. However, she knows that the task at hand can be daunting. Therefore, she should prepare a series of sub-goals to help her get to the overall goal of passing her exam and finally obtain her license. She may produce the following sub-goals:

1. Arrange for an eye exam to ensure that she can safely drive a vehicle.

2. Attend a safe driving course.

3. Work with a driving instructor to increase her proficiency.

4. Divide the process of learning to drive based on various situations she might enter into. These include situations like highway driving, tight urban situations, parking, and even when she has to get off of a road.

All these sub-goals will make it easier for her to be aware of what she is going to do to get her license. By using these sub-goals, Kim will have more control over what she wants to do to complete her tasks.

Review the Triggers

The triggers that make a situation worse must be explored. It is through these triggers that depression or other emotional concerns might develop. In Kim's case, she might have triggers relating to what might happen when driving. She might be worried about what happens while on a highway or when she is trying to park the car.

She would have to plan her studies for getting her license by spacing her lessons based on certain tasks. She might focus on the basics of driving at the start and get used to regular road situations through instruction. After a while, she will go on to work on her highway driving skills. As she becomes more used to handling a car, the triggers that come with getting on the highway or trying to park will start to disappear. This all comes as she will no longer feel worried or nervous about what she is doing.

Successive approximations help to keep the triggers one has at bay. The triggers will become weak when the right plans to address them are met and attained. This will require extra effort on a person's part, and that includes using the appropriate sub-goals. The triggers for each stage should be identified before the task is attempted. This is to figure out the problems that one might have.

Decide Where to Start

People will be less likely to feel depressed or worried when they know how to start their efforts to improve themselves. The key for this part of the process is to look at where one can go when trying to start something new and figure out a smart plan for attack. For Kim, she knows that her starting point would be to attend a class to learn to drive and to get her eye exam to ensure she can handle driving. This helps her feel confident in what she is doing. At this point, she knows that she is on the right track. Those who know how to start a task will not likely feel upset or worried about what they are doing. Those people will feel excited and ready to take on anything that might happen.

Progressively Move Forward Through the Goals

The goals that were established at the start should be followed. Planning one's way through these goals is a necessity. The efforts needed must be measured appropriately and with enough care to see that one moves forward toward the main goal. Kim would use the sub-goals as a guide map for going forward. She will replace the fears and depressed feelings she had of not knowing what to do with a concrete idea for how she is going to make her work in learning to drive a success. Kim has the options to use as many of these goals as she wants. It would take more time for her to get through the situation if she has more goals to work with.

After Everything Is Finished

As Kim finally gets her driver's license, she feels confident in knowing that she can go on the open road and enjoy everything the world has to offer. Her depressed feelings will be kept in control as she feels more positive about her ability to drive. This point about successive approximations is something that anyone can use. After the task is finished, the issues that caused someone to become depressed are reduced. This makes life easier and reduces the panic that one might have.

How Much Time?

Successive approximations are needed to help people accomplish complicated tasks that might seem overwhelming. The process should only take whatever amount of time one needs. This could take weeks to complete, or even months depending on how intense or difficult the task might be. However, the task at hand should be planned accordingly based on what someone knows they are capable of accomplishing.

Chapter 38 – Anger and How CBT Corrects the Situation

Anger is a problem that many people feel at times and is also a concern that makes it harder for a person to get along with other people. It is an emotion that everyone is bound to feel at some point. Anger can be triggered by just about anything. The anger someone holds might be due to something that just does not go that person's way. It might come from another person having something positive happen while the person who is angry did not receive any benefits. Anger is a concern that can permeate one's life and trigger feelings of frustration. It is critical for people to understand what they can do to handle certain problems relating to anger.

Recognizing the Body's Response to Anger

Anger is a problem that will cause the body to respond in a unique fashion. Some of the things that will happen within the body include the following:

- An angry person's body will start to release adrenaline. This is a hormone that causes muscles to tighten while the heart rate increases.

- The amygdala in the brain will be triggered to cause significant frustrations and anger in one's mind.

- The body's senses might become more sensitive. They will be more likely to notice some of the unpleasant things and triggers.

- The skin may also appear flushed, although this is primarily due to the increased heart rate and body temperature that accompanies anger.

The frustration that comes with anger can be dramatic. It is through one's ability to handle anger that it might be easier for a situation to be resolved. Knowing what causes anger can be significant.

What Causes Anger?

Anger is a frustrating feeling, but it is something that must be explored to understand it. There are many things that might cause anger:

- Certain triggers in one's mind are going to cause a person to become angry. These include triggers that focus on things one does not like.

- Situations where something does not go a person's way can be dramatic. In many cases, a trigger might develop when someone makes a plan for the day but ends up losing control of those plans.

- Traumatic memories may also be a trigger. There are often times when outside sources might cause someone to become angry and incapable of controlling one's mind.

- One's individual history can contribute to feelings of anger. The past events or the attitudes or biases one holds might cause anger to become worse.

The threat of anger is significant in that a person who becomes angry will be harder to manage and communicate with.

Acknowledging the Anger

There are many things that can be done using CBT-related functions. Watch how the anger is being handled in one's mind. Anyone who keeps in one's anger might struggle with keeping one's body under control. When anger comes into one's mind, the pains and sensations that someone might feel may become worse and harder to control. Suppressing anger is only going to make the situation more difficult. So, how can the anger be expressed without taking it out on someone? The best thing to do is to recognize the anger and notice that the feeling is developing.

Be aware of the angry situation and make some self-statements that recognize what is happening. For instance, an angry person might say something like, "My heart rate is starting to go up" or "Whatever is going on here is not what I intended to have happened." Be willing to address the anger, but do not project the anger outward toward other people. Having a sense of control over how the anger is handled will help anyone to manage one's mind. Considering the anger in question and acknowledging its presence can go a long way toward helping a person manage the issues that caused the anger.

Review the Anger

After acknowledging the anger directly, it is time to review that anger. Look at the issue that caused the anger to develop and ask a few questions:

1. What are the positives associated with responding in anger?

There might be times when anger will cause someone to feel relieved or feel a little more in control.

2. What are the negatives?

Anger might also cause a person to feel embarrassed by having one's attitude or hostility exposed in a negative light.

3. Is this anger something that happens all the time?

The anger might be something that someone experienced a while ago and continues to occur.

4. What could have caused the anger to develop? Was it something that was unnecessary and trivial?

Short vs. Long-Term Help

Another way to review the anger is to look at the short and long-term effects of being angry. The anger one experiences might be a feeling of relief in a brief moment as expressing that anger allows for some release. The long-term effects could be harmful. Being angry might cause other people to judge someone in a negative light. The anger may also cause other people to also feel anger even if they had nothing to do with the situation at the time. Examining the problems that have occurred should help understand that there are some positives involved with being angry, but those are not going to do much to help someone down the line.

Be Removed From the Situation

The situation that caused someone to become angry might be hard to manage if someone remains in that situation. It is through direct communication with the issue that someone's angry might become even stronger. Let's use an example of Ken and how he might become angry because of some accounting task not working as well as hoped. He might have thought that he was doing things right, but it turns out that he was wasting his time on the whole thing. He thought too much about certain processes and ended up failing to make the task work out right. As a result, his boss is angry with him.

Ken would also be angry and would probably complain to his boss about it if he wanted to. At this point, it might be easier for him to feel frustrated due to how he spent all that time trying to manage the work that he wanted to complete. The best thing for Ken to do at this point is to get away from the situation for a few minutes. He can step out of the office for about five to ten minutes to clear his mind. Maybe he could get a bit of fresh air outdoors.

After spending a bit of time collecting his thoughts, Ken can talk to his boss about the situation. He will feel more at ease as he will have a little more control over what he is thinking. He could start talking to his boss about what he did wrong and what he thought at the start. After that, the two can devise a plan to alleviate the situation and fix the problem. By getting away from the situation, Ken was able to tackle the issue again. He got over the anger and realized that he can fix the problem.

Consider the Alternatives

Being rational and reasonable is an essential part of CBT that no one should ignore. This is surely the case with managing anger. The alternative solutions to a problem can be explored in detail to see if something good can be done to keep a problem from becoming worse. In Ken's case, he would have looked at the alternatives of what he had been doing after he got mad. As he worked to calm himself down, he thought about the things that he could have done instead of becoming angry. In this case, Ken decided that he would have to talk to his boss about the situation to determine what went wrong so it issue can be resolved.

Practice Happiness or Positive Thinking

A person who becomes angry must be willing to practice happiness or think a little differently about what one wants to attain out of life and have more control over situations that could occur.

A few points can be used in this process:

1. Observe the angry feelings that one has.

2. Identify the source of the anger.

3. Look at the problem is and find a positive way to spin the issue.

In Ken's example, he might notice from his work that he can learn from the errors that he made. He can concentrate on ways to correct the problem and keep it from coming up again. By turning the problem into a learning experience, he will feel happy knowing that he is doing something for himself without having to be hard on anyone else.

4. Release the original negative thought that occurred. Remove that old thought and replace it with the new positive spin on things.

Anger can be a dramatic issue and it is vital for people who are angry to see what they can do to manage the situations that they encounter. Knowing what can be done to keep anger from being a serious threat or dangerous concern to one's emotions helps to improve upon one's life while also helping someone to see that there are many ways how the anger could be corrected or controlled.

Chapter 39 – Managing Grief Through CBT

Grief is one of the most difficult emotions that any person could ever experience and it is an emotion that all people will have to face at some point in their lives. No one can ever live forever, which makes it all the more essential to understand how to control one's grief and how to stay positive even when a person reaches one's darkest hour in life. Grief is a feeling that develops when a person is in a deep state of sadness. This is different from depression in that grief is typically caused not by life in general but rather by a very specific event. In most cases, grief is triggered by the death of a loved one. Whether it is the loss of a parent, a sibling, a close friend, or even a family pet, grief is painful.

The Basics and the Classic Five Stages

Grief is an emotion where a person is in deep despair and sadness as a result of a painful experience. The feelings that someone develops as a result of one's grief are often pervasive.

To fully understand grief, it helps to understand how it progresses. There are five stages of grief.

1. Denial

In the beginning, a person is not going to want to believe that someone has died or something irreversible has happened. This might all seem like a terrible dream, but in reality, it is indeed happening.

2. Anger

Sometimes that anger is directed at people who could not do anything to resolve a problem. It may also come from one's inability to correct the situation.

   3. Bargaining

The bargaining will be unsuccessful as that person goes through more emotional pain and stress than what one might be capable of bearing.

   4. Depression

A person will experience deep depression after realizing that the grief is real and that nothing can be done to rectify it. This is the stage where the intense and difficult sorrow has to be endured.

   5. Acceptance

Eventually, a person will begin to accept that the grief is indeed real. It will be time to get over the situation and to finally be at peace with what has happened. This is the ultimate goal of the grief cycle. In some cases, it might be difficult for a person to finally reach the stage of acceptance. The amount of time it takes for a person to manage the situation can vary.

The Three Main Types of Grief

People experience grief in different ways. One way to understand this is by looking at the three basic types of grief that a person might experience.

   1. Acute Grief

Acute grief occurs right after a loss and will go on for weeks or even months. People may have feelings of distress, shock, sadness, and even an inability to sleep. The effects of acute grief will disappear after a while.

2. Complicated Grief

Complicated grief occurs when the acute grief is not lessening. It may take years for the grief to subside. As the grief remains, it becomes harder for a person to feel happy. A person might start to feel guilty if they cannot move on from the grief.

3. Integrated Grief

Integrated grief will last throughout one's life and is not going to disappear. Integrated grief shows that a person still misses someone and will always grieve, but at the same time that person will have accepted the loss and understood that it will eventually be time to move on. The problem with integrated grief is that it will often produce reminders of one's loss at varying times throughout life. This might happen when someone visits a place where their loved one died or some other place that holds significance for personal reasons. The grief may also appear during anniversaries and holidays relating to one's life. The concern surrounding these forms of grief is that there is never a way for someone to truly get over the loss of a loved one. Although a person might appear to have got past the grief, there will always be repressed memories or thoughts attached to that person.

Common Effects That Accompany Grief

The signs that accompany one's feelings of grief can be frustrating and often hard to live with. They can be:

- Feelings of separation may develop after having lost someone.

- Crying and sorrow can happen at random because a person is not capable of managing one's emotions or might not be in the strongest of states.

- Hallucinations might develop in some people who struggle with grief. Such hallucinations focus on things relating to the person that a person has lost.

- Sleeping issues may also develop. A person might not be able to get to sleep because that someone is too busy thinking about all that has been lost.

Using CBT to Handle Grief

The following are steps that may be used when handling someone's grief by using cognitive behavioral therapy.

1. Start by addressing the thoughts that a person has about the grief.

The thoughts that someone has surrounding grief may present as anger or denial at the beginning. The key is to help a person address the anger or other hostile feelings that one might have begun to have. Look at what caused the anger to develop. The odds are that anger is something that came about not from one's hostility but rather from the sadness. It is through one's feelings of helplessness that the anger develops.

2. Review the perception as a result of the grief.

Every person perceives grief in different ways. Some people might see grief as something that is a way of life, but others might feel that it is unnatural or embarrassing. The key is to replace the attitude one has and look at examples of how people grieve. By using this alongside the rationalization one has of one's grief, it becomes easier for a person to stop feeling excessively worried about grieving.

3. Think about the attitudes that one might have surrounding the grief.

The attitudes that are produced as a result of one's grief should be inspected. This includes a review of the problems that have happened because of the grief. A person should look at the situation and note the emotions one is feeling. Find relationships between each of these things to understand of what might be happening in one's life.

4. Be grounded in the present.

The attitudes in one's mind should be organized based on how grounded they might be. The goal is to look at how the mind is handling the loss and what someone might have to consider following the event.

A good way to work with CBT is to think about present thoughts and plan for goals of what one can do. The present mood may be analyzed and then adjusted over time to stay happy and in control over one's emotional state.

5. Avoid trying to keep emotions inside.

This is a part of therapy that cannot be expressed enough. Anyone who keeps their emotions inside without being able to express them could be at risk of harm as the mind struggles to maintain a sense of control and peace. These basic steps may work alongside various additional exercises such as the ones that are listed in this chapter. These include points that help someone to keep one's thoughts organized and to develop a sense of recognition of whatever someone is thinking during a period of grief.

Preparing a Goodbye Worksheet

Saying goodbye to someone is often difficult, but it is through this that a person can move forward in the cognitive psychology process. A goodbye worksheet may be used as a guide to analyzing the feelings that someone has developed after losing a loved one. A goodbye worksheet is a CBT exercise that focuses on how well a person can respond to a situation. A worksheet should include the following:

1. Explain why someone is saying goodbye. This might be because of someone's death.

2. Explain what it feels like to say goodbye. This is where the emotions of grief can be revealed and the person will become familiar with the worries they are harboring.

3. Describe some good memories of the person who has died. This may help add some peace or comfort in one's mind as the past is recalled and a person feels a little better by remembering happy situations.

4. Write down something that one would have wanted to say to someone who died. This allows for more of one's emotions to be revealed.

5. Explain something that one will always remember about that person.

These questions are often difficult to answer at times, but they are ones that should be addressed as honestly and carefully as possible to show one's appreciation for the other person.

Be Willing to Forgive

One exercise involves a desire to forgive. There might have been times when someone was wrong or harsh on other people for whatever reason. These include cases where someone might have disagreed with others or could have been critical of one's life in general. The goal of this exercise is to improve the mood by being willing to forgive:

1. Talk with others who have been wronged in the past. These include others who were related to the person who died.

2. Explain to others about the concerns that one has. This includes the feelings that one held in the past as a result of one's attitudes.

3. Be open about what is happening. Explain that there is nothing wrong with a situation and that it is helpful to talk with others.

4. Listen to the other person in the situation. Be willing to recognize the impact that one's words have. The person does indeed have power over the things one wishes to say or think.

Be Willing to Forgive the Self

In addition to forgiving other people, a person who struggles with grief must also forgive themselves. There might have been some unresolved issues with the person who died. Maybe that person did not have the opportunity to tell that person something important or even a secret that could have been shared. The self should be forgiven by acknowledging what one might have done in the past while thinking about what could have been said. This helps a person to look back at one's life and recognize that maybe some of the more difficult or trivial things that one thought about were not all that critical and do not have to cause a person to be overly judgmental.

Invite New Things into One's Life

Much of CBT has been about replacing negative ideas with positive ones. This can surely be said about grief as it helps to replace the grief over time with something new in one's life. It is a good idea to invite something new into one's life to create a sense of positivity or comfort.

There are many things that can be done to replace the feelings of sorrow:

- Take part in some new hobbies or activities. Such new things might be more entertaining for someone to consider.

- Travel to someplace that produces positive memories or even somewhere that one has never been to before. See what makes it an outstanding area for someone to visit and enjoy relaxation.

- Bring a new plant into the house. Having something to take care of and to honor someone with is always a smart idea.

- Consider adopting a new pet to care for. A pet will give unconditionally love and will always provide good company.

The varying things that can be done to alleviate grief can be worthwhile and should make one's life positive. It is through this positivity that it becomes easier for a person to avoid the problems that come with grief and to get closer to finally reaching that state of acceptance.

Emphasize Positive Memories

The last thing to do for managing grief is to look back at the positive memories that someone had with a person that was lost. This might be difficult at times because it often involves some of the things that one might never be able to experience again. Thinking about those positive memories should make it easier for that person to feel happy about the time one spent together.

There are some things one can do:

1. Address any negative thoughts surrounding one's grief.

2. Find a positive memory that relates to the negative thought. This could be a trip or other experience that a person had with the other person.

3. Reflect on the memory with care. Look at some of the good things that took place within that memory.

4. Allow that memory to leave the mind. The good memory should have overwhelmed the negative thought at this point.

Performing this practice regularly helps a person to habitually manage the feelings that one has and to keep the harmful thoughts that could develop from being a dramatic threat to one's happiness. Keeping negative thoughts from being a burden in one's life can help ease the pain and worry that might develop as a result of the thoughts that are permeating one's mind. The positive memories that one has produced throughout life and the things that anyone can reflect upon are always worth exploring and thinking about when finding a way to be happy. Those who wish to get the most out of their lives and avoid the negative things that come with grief and sorrow can look back with fondness at these memories and know that there is something worth recalling.

An Essential Note

As valuable as CBT can be to handle grief, it is important to avoid rushing a person into a plan to get over one's mental or emotional struggles. Being able to move on and handle the grief in question is not something that anyone can do immediately. It might take time for a person to do this. The best thing to do when dealing with someone who is struck with grief is to allow that person to have some time to think about the situation. Whatever the case may be, it is important to be gentle and supportive of any person who might have a hard time with managing their grief. The use of CBT is vital for managing one's life and keeping grief from being a serious problem, but it should all be done responsibly and with respect for the person who needs the help.

Chapter 40 – The Art of Journaling

People love to be creative. They love to come up with many unique things they want to produce. Whether it is writing, performing music, drawing, or another activity, there are many ways people can produce creative things and express their ideas in ways that they might have never thought about before. One such way people can do this is through journaling. Journaling is a very self-explanatory practice that anyone can use. It is a practice where a person will write various things in a book with all of the points relating to what someone has done on a typical day. This is a practice that has been used by people of all sorts and all ages because of how easy it can be to produce a distinct story.

Journaling may work well for people who are trying to handle their fears, feelings of depression, or the grief that they may feel. The steps of the journal are essential to review. In fact, this may work exceptionally well to identify when someone is experiencing some kind of fear that makes it harder for the body to respond and feel comfortable.

Creating a Journal

While traditional journaling involves writing about the things that one did during the course of a day, CBT journaling focuses on identifying how well certain values or ideas might be produced.

1. Write about the activating event that is experienced that day.

The activating event is a situation that leads to feeling something unpleasant. The person might include details on the fears that one felt, the grief someone experienced, and so forth. The journal entry should include the place where the situation occurred, when it happened, how long the issue lasted, and who was involved. The situation should be explained with as many details as possible.

2. Think about the initial thought that occurred during the activating event.

Discuss the first thing that came into one's mind. These can be automatic thoughts or just something that comes out subconsciously.

3. Look at the negative beliefs that were produced.

Depression, grief, and other negative beliefs often come from equally negative thoughts. The negative thoughts should be discussed in detail while also explaining the source of that thought. Sometimes the thinking might come about because of one event that happened in the past. Maybe it was an interaction with someone else. There has to be some intense belief that is driving the negative thoughts that have occurred.

4. Think about the consequences of the negative thought.

Every negative idea has some problems associated if the issue is not resolved. Short and long-term consequences may be produced if the negative attitude persists for too long. Such problems might include harm to one's mind, body, and relationships if the problematic issue is not resolved. Knowing the consequences may motivate a person to change one's mind and attitude. Not resolving those problems will only make one's life worse as the anxieties and other concerns one has will persist.

5. Review the arguments both for and against the negative thinking.

There has to be a closer look taken at what might be causing someone to have certain attitudes or values. For instance, someone might have been in the same situation in the past and could have felt the same way. A review of what happened as a result and the lessons learned helps to understand the concerns that someone has.

6. After reviewing the negative thinking, devise a new way of thinking.

The review of the negative thinking should be an analysis of what can be done to keep a situation from being worse.

7. Plan an affirmation.

An affirmation is a saying that encourages a person to have a happier and more productive life. This statement can include anything, but it should focus on how positive someone's life can be provided a new strategy is used.

8. Establish an action plan.

The action plan is a new strategy to resolve a problem in the future. The action plan can include any kind of change or attitude, but it must involve something realistic. The new plan must be simple and create a more productive and positive effect.

9. The next time the situation occurs, write down a new journal entry explaining the things that were done this time. Take note of the improvements that took place.

The analysis should include a review of how a problem was resolved and how better one's mind was as a result. These steps can help people change their lives.

An Example of Journaling

To fully recognize how this process works, a full example is needed. Let's look at the story of Tony. He is a high school student who has struggled to complete public speeches. He often is overcome by worry. Tony wants to improve upon his ability to make a speech. He wants to be free of the anxiety that develops when trying to make a speech, not to mention the anger that evolves from failing. Therefore, he will produce a journal to make it easier for him to decide what he can do for himself.

1. Tony would write about how he had a difficult time trying to complete a presentation in the classroom. He would explain in as much detail as possible how difficult the speech was and what he tried to do to save face.

2. The first thoughts that Tony had should be cataloged next. He must explain these feelings no matter how intense or deep they might have been.

3. The root of his thinking should be explored. He must think about prior events before that led to similar feelings.

4. By analyzing the consequences of the event, Tony will notice that he needs to make a change. He knows that his grade and his social standing could both be hurt if he does not keep his mind under control.

5. Tony will then determine why he feels his responses were worthwhile. As he looks at how he was unhappy or upset with his speech, he will start to notice that those feelings will only cause him to become even more frustrated or upset.

6. Next, Tony considers new ways to think about his speeches. He would realize that people in the classroom might be more receptive if he focused more on the speech as a whole rather than struggling with just one aspect.

7. Tony will write an affirmation that he is capable of doing anything if he focuses on what he wants to do.

8. The next actions that Tony thought about just a moment ago should be used during the next speech he makes. He may look at the entire speech and focus on being well-rounded instead of just focusing on one thing. He would also be less judgmental of himself when looking at how people respond to his speech.

9. After his next speech, he will add an entry to his journal. He may explain that he felt better and more confident about the speech that he just made.

Tony must think carefully about how he's going to respond to a certain situation and how he will plan his future moves. By using his journal, Tony will notice the mental processes he is using and how they are dictating what he does with his speeches. This gives him a better chance of handling his future speeches. People who engage in journaling for CBT will be impressed with how well the process can work. It is through journaling that a person can get closer to one's attitudes and values. Having a clear idea of what one might be thinking will make a real difference in one's work.

What Types of Topics Can Be Covered In a Journal?

The best part of journaling for CBT is that the practice can be about any subject matter. To make the journal worthwhile, it helps to be realistic or sensible.

For instance, a person might have a desire to write about ways how someone can resolve certain financial issues. For instance, a person might think about going back to school to increase the ability to earn money. This is a realistic plan. A person might also write about winning the lottery or having an inheritance from a family member. Although those are interesting aspects of managing financial problems, they are not realistic. The overall goal is to instill a sense of hope in one's life. Finding ways to make the mind feel happier and stronger is the primary goal.

Chapter 41 – Forming Alternative Actions

Much of this guide has focused on taking a look at alternative actions that can be used to correct the problems that one has encountered. This chapter concentrates on a process to find the correct alternative actions that may be used.

1. List the problems and difficulties that one might be having.

Let's look at Janet and how she is having a hard time managing a relationship with her boyfriend. Janet might be worried that her relationship is not going well. Janet might list many problems and difficulties that she has in that relationship. She might state there is a lack of intimacy or that she's too nervous to take that next step with him.

2. List the vulnerabilities of a situation.

In Janet's situation, she might state that she experiences problems in her relationship when she goes out in public with her boyfriend.

3. Triggers have to be directed toward the problems and difficulties.

The triggers, in this case, are the situations that make things worse. Janet might write that one of the triggers of her nervousness is when she is not properly dressed for a date.

4. After defining the problems, a series of coping strategies can be produced.

The coping strategies listed are not designed to be definite solutions to the problem. Rather, they are to help people find ways to cope with the problems that they might be struggling with. Such coping strategies should be used to help someone feel better, even if this happens temporarily. Janet might plan to do exercises for relaxing or meditating. She might talk to herself and think about what she wishes to do. Knowing how to manage one's emotions in this situation should be explored carefully.

5. The effects of the coping strategies that were produced should be listed next.

The coping process could take as long as it needs to depending on how well a person can respond to the process. Talking over one's feelings or worries with other people is always a good idea to ensure that one's mind can be kept positive and organized.

6. A series of alternative actions may be listed.

The new actions that can be used in a task should be explored. This strategy for managing alternative actions does not have to be difficult. Great ideas might come about when trying to replace difficult thoughts.

Chapter 42 – The Validity Test

Validity refers to how accurate something might be. Something that is false might be interpreted as being true. The validity test involves a combination of the CBT strategies that have been listed in this guide plus journaling. Consider the new thoughts that one has developed to correct negative thoughts. The goal is to review each of these thoughts to decide which ones are working best.

There are several steps that may be used to test for validity:

1. Think about the negative thought that was introduced.

For this example, let's look at Susan and her desire to lose weight. She might have a negative thought like "It is very difficult for me to lose weight." She would try to resolve her weight issues, but she is uncertain as to what she can do. Susan must replace that negative thought with a positive one.

2. The negative thought should have been replaced with a positive thought.

The CBT process helps someone find something easy and realistic to follow. Susan's case could include a positive thought like "I can lose weight by cutting down on sugary foods."

3. A secondary positive thought should be included.

Susan might come up with a statement like "I need to get more exercise each week to help me lose weight."

4. A journal should be kept to see how valid these two thoughts are.

The journaling process records the thoughts one had during the day and how they were acted upon. Susan would use her journal to regularly record what she was doing when trying to use these positive thoughts. She might state which of the two thoughts she used and then decide how well she was able to abide by one of those. For instance, Susan might have used her belief that avoiding sugary foods is best on Monday and Wednesday. She would look at how well she managed to live a healthy life based on what she is recording in her journal. She might state that she was able to avoid sugary foods and that she had more energy throughout the day.

Meanwhile, she might have also used the idea about being more active and getting extra exercise on Tuesdays and Thursdays. She would have used this to try to have more exercise and be physical while still managing a healthy diet. She could also list in her journal that she did not manage her diet very well on those days.

5. Compare the results of those two thoughts based on what was recorded in the journal.

In Susan's case, she did much better on Mondays and Wednesdays when her main focus was to avoid sugary foods. She not only had a better diet but also found she had more energy to help her keep active. Susan did not do so well on those other two days when she was trying to exercise. She might have got tired after all that work, thus keeping her from thinking twice about the foods she was eating. The struggles that she had proved that the first thought she had was better.

Susan found through the validity test that her first thought was the most valid of the two as it was easier for her to follow and also produced the best results to feel healthy and in control of her body. This test helped Susan to collect the data she needed to see which of the positive thoughts she was using was best. By using the one that she knows will work, it will be easier for her to stay with a healthy routine.

How Many Variables?

The validity test can work with many variables. The goal is to keep those variables linked to the same end goal that one wishes to reach. At least two or three variables should be compared when getting one's cognitive issues under control. By using a few variables, it should be easier for problems to be corrected. In the example, Susan used two variables – the first was avoiding sugary foods and the second was exercise. She could add a third variable like to drink more water during the day and maybe a fourth variable regarding adding fiber to her diet. She could use all of these on alternating days and write down the results for each of these things.

How Much Time Is Needed?

The validity test can continue for as long as one wants. It is best to have a few weeks of work to determine how well a task is being handled. In Susan's case, she might have to work on testing those two variables for about a month to see what happens. She can record information on how well she is living by the points covered in her test. She can notice that she is putting in a great deal of effort into her plan for losing weight.

The potential for the validity test to generate real results is worth trying.

What If the Idea Is Invalid?

There are times when some feeling or action might be deemed invalid and an alternative needs to be implemented. Instead of just shrugging off the invalid idea, it might be best to come up with a new solution that may be used to resolve the invalid idea and to find a suitable alternative.

1. Look at what has caused a suggestion or idea to be invalid. Discover why it is illogical or not working.

2. Think about the invalid action and compare it with the goal.

3. Find a similar solution that may be used instead. Find something that works with the plans one might have had in mind.

Figuring out a smart plan for handling an invalid idea only takes a few moments to complete.

Chapter 43 – The Art of Visualization

Visualization is a practice where someone creates a visual representation of something that a person might be thinking about. This could be anything from a look back at something a person did or what someone might be thinking about doing in the future. Visualization can be used to resolve certain problems. For instance, a person might think about something one wishes to do and then play back in one's mind a routine that can be used to accomplish that task. Visualization provides a person the opportunity to see things in a whole new light.

The methods learned in this guide about replacing negative thoughts with good ones can be used in a visualization process to manage certain concepts or values. The best part of using visualization is that it is a process that works for any need. Anyone can utilize visualization to control one's thoughts and to stay comfortable with whatever one might be doing. In fact, practically anything can be visualized in the process as long as it is positive and produces a better end result when thinking about what can happen.

The example is about Jake, a writer who is looking to make progress on his new manuscript. He will wake up in the morning and think about what he can do to manage his task and make it easier for him to write. He will use visualization to review what he wants to do and how he will make it work.

How to Use Visualization

Let's start looking at Jake's example to see how visualization will work for him.

1. Start by visualizing how the day will start.

After waking up, it is imperative to decide what will happen that day. For Jake, he will have to look at how he is going to work that day. He will visualize himself waking up, having a shower, enjoying breakfast, and then working on his manuscript for a few hours. He might think about specific things about his book that he wants to work on.

2. While visualizing, make everything as positive as possible.

Visualization should be done using positive thoughts and feelings. This allows a person to feel better about the work one is planning to do. Jake will think about the progress he will make in his book. He will visualize himself doing more work on his book and creating connections or even editing his outline. He will manage his work based on what he thinks is suitable and easy.

3. Identify anything negative that might occur.

Although visualization is about positivity, it is important to watch for anything negative that appears. It is natural for people to have fears and worries about what they will do, but identifying anything that might take place is essential. Jake might be worried about the power going out in his home. Jake knows that the weather report says that storms are expected. Anything like this would cause him to worry about missing a deadline or otherwise losing his train of thought while working. Jake has to look at this potential and see what he can do to resolve the fear he has. Knowing what he can do for controlling something as negative as this will help him to keep himself from being bothered.

4. Find a way to place a positive outcome on something negative.

After a negative thought comes about, a plan should be used to resolve the worries or issues that someone might have. Jake would think about the potential for the power to go off and Jake would look at how he can resolve the issue. He might consider alternative actions like writing notes on paper about what he will do in the event that the power does go out. He might also consider planning an email that can be written in the event the power does go out. This email could explain to a client that there is a weather-related issue that would cause him to miss a deadline.

Jake would resolve that negative thought he had with a new belief. He will know that there is something he can do in the event the worst case scenario does happen. He will continue to feel positive and not afraid of what might happen. Jake would keep on working while knowing in the back of his mind that nothing bad will happen and that he has a plan if something disruptive does happen. Jake can focus all of his attention on the work he had planned for the day. He will be ready to do whatever it is he had planned and will not be afraid of disruptions. This newfound development will lessen his fears or be frustrated.

5. Later, the person should look back at the day and note everything that happened. This includes a look at all the positive as well as the negative things.

An analysis of how the day went and how someone responded to the problem should be noted. Jake would use this step to review how well he did with his manuscript. He may also notice that while he was highly productive, he still has a few loose ends in his work that needs to be resolved. He will visualize how he is going to resolve those problems. The most important part of this step is that Jake is finding a way to manage the negative things. He is using positive thinking and functions to resolve the mental worries he has. This gives him extra control over what he wishes to do and how he will feel better about the work he is doing.

6. Before the end of the day, a plan for what will happen the following day should be determined. Any negative worries must be addressed and cataloged.

Part of this might include deciding if that negative thought was logical or not. He will visualize what he will do tomorrow and how much time he has for doing it. While planning his next day, a negative thought might enter into Jake's mind. In this case, he might worry that his client will want him to change the rules he is following to complete his task. He fears the client will demand too much and that the goals he set for a task would change dramatically.

Jake will review the issue based on how much of a change would take place and whether or not the client would realistically ask for a certain change. After acknowledging the issue, he might determine that the problem in question would not be much of a threat to him. He will start to feel that the problems might not be that serious or that there is a realistic way for him to answer the concerns. Visualization is a valuable and essential task. The steps listed here are designed to help anyone with getting the most out of the work one puts in to managing thoughts and planning something that is not hard to follow or use in life.

Chapter 44 – An Exercise in Positive Thinking

Cognitive behavioral therapy helps people to restore the positive feelings they have had, but there is one other exercise that may be used alongside CBT to help improve upon one's thinking and develop positive ideas. This process works alongside the virtues of perception and attention. By using this exercise, a person will find ways to perceive positive things in a situation and to also pay attention to whatever might result.

Three Simple Steps

This process should only take a few moments to complete:

1. Look at the surroundings at one point in the day.

It could be inside one's home, inside a classroom, or in a workplace. Every space is conducive for supporting this exercise.

2. Look around the area to find at least five positive things.

Regardless of the scene, there is always bound to be something good to notice. Look around to find as many good things as possible so there remains a sense of positivity in whatever is happening.

3. Try this practice again later on in the day. Keep as consistent of a schedule for doing this as possible.

This practice can be done as many times as wanted. Doing this at the same time each day or night is the best idea as it allows someone to create a healthy habit of noticing all the good things. It is through the sense of optimism that it becomes easier for an issue to be resolved.

An Example

First, someone might wake up at 6:30 in the morning and eventually notice what is outside. That person might notice that it is raining. Many people might assume that the day is going to be gloomy and dreary, but better and smarter thoughts can be produced. For instance, five good things can be said about the rainy day:

1. The rain will water all the plants.
2. The rain will produce a rainbow at the end of it all.
3. The streets are still easy to navigate.
4. All that pollen or any other bits of dirt left on a pavement will be washed away.
5. The sky is not too bright and it will be easy to drive to work.

Each of these points is designed to be comfortable and easy on one's mind. After a while, the person can plan another session.

What If a Negative Thought Occurs?

There is always the chance that a negative thought will interfere. Look back at the issue and think about a positive secondary thought. Let's go back to the situation on a rainy day. Someone might start to think about how the rain might cause flooding on the streets. A new positive thought can be used relating to that point. Instead of thinking that the streets will be flooded, a person might think that the drainage system on the road is working well, thus ensuring the roads will still be easy to navigate. The most important thing to do is to never suppress such negative thoughts. There is always going to be a chance that such a negative opinion will come about while thinking about things.

When Does This Work?

Be sure to following this exercise a few times a day for the best results to have positive thinking. Completing this process at a set time in the day is the best thing that someone can consider for having a better sense of control over life. The main objective is to find a way to incorporate the practice into one's daily life.

Chapter 45 – Reframing Disappointment

There is always a time when someone might be upset or unhappy. A person might hope that one event will go in a certain direction and be disappointed. Disappointment occurs when someone is engaged in an activity and something difficult happens. Perhaps that person might notice that one's skills are not as good as they should be. The biggest problem with disappointment is that it makes a person feel like a failure. A person can be quickly depressed when one feels disappointed. People should not get too upset when they are disappointed. The feeling of disappointment is generally fleeting.

Make It Normal

The best way to reframe disappointment is to make it feel as though it is a normal part of life. This aspect of cognitive psychology gives the person the feeling that there is no need to feel depressed or down when things don't go one's way. The fact of the matter is that everyone is going to be disappointed about something at some point in life. It only makes sense to take that feeling of disappointment and keep it from being far too intense or extreme. It is important to know how to keep the difficult feeling at bay without fear or concern.

Disappointment can be resolved by:

1. Review the things that contributed to the disappointing situation.

The things that contribute to a situation can be divided into two subsections. First, the problems at a time might be produced due to the one's own actions. Second, the problems might be from things that are out of one's control.

2. The things that someone was not in control of having to be discarded.

If the situation was out of one's control, it is best to discard those problems.

3. Review the things that one contributed to directly. Decide how those issues can be resolved in the future.

The third step concentrates on replacing the negative feelings one has with positive feelings surrounding what can be done in the future. New ways of acting including solutions for resolving problems can be planned. For example, Tony is not able to make it to a family dinner. He might have been disappointed because he really wanted to attend the special event so he could have some quality time with his family members. For whatever reason, he might not have been able to make it.

He would list the reasons why he could not attend the dinner:

- His day at the workplace lasted slightly longer than he wanted. There might have been no opportunity for him to leave work early that day.

- Tony might have also struggled with traffic on the way to the dinner.

- He might also have been working a little too hard to find the right wardrobe for the event. He could have taken too much time going through his wardrobe and he lost track of time.

Tony would have to analyze each of these things to see what he could have done differently. He could discard the second issue because he could not control the traffic situation. Tony would notice that he had a role in some of the problems. He was unable to leave work sooner. He could have planned his working day better to allow leaving work in time to make the dinner date. The third problem is also something he could easily control. He might learn from this experience that he needs to be a little more assertive and definitive when finding what he wishes to wear for an event. The decisions that Tony makes at this point will help him to manage his life a little better without worrying about getting into any further problems. He needs to make better plans.

The Main Goal

Being able to manage one's feelings of disappointment helps to keep from feeling overly upset about what one might be trying to do and being capable of controlling one's feelings. It is not healthy to feel disappointed for too long. Using the exercise listed in this chapter helps a person avoid prolonged feelings of disappointment, thus making it easier for that someone to feel confident and at ease with whatever someone might try to do at a time.

Chapter 45 – Final Tips for CBT

The many things that have been covered in this guide deserve to be noticed. However, there are a few final tips that need to be discussed when aiming to get the most out of the cognitive behavioral therapy process.

Always Have a Goal

A clear-cut goal will include a clear objective. The goal can be anything that someone one wants to do so long as it is reasonable and positive. The goal can be a short or long-term one as well. The goal must be clearly defined and realistic regardless of the type of situation that one encounters.

Every Situation Is Unique

Overgeneralization and other distortions are often things that people will encounter. These problems often make it harder for people to plan smart ideas or thoughts. People need to recognize that the situations are always different. People might look at the circumstances including a review of each situation based on the setting, the people who are involved, and any other things that might trigger changes. People should avoid personalizing the situations. Personalizing can disrupt one's train of thought. Don't assume everything is about oneself.

Determine the Proper Definitions

Every attitude or emotion that one has will come with a distinct definition. It is up to a person to recognize the certain definitions that one wishes to follow when figuring out how well CBT can work. For instance, a person might have one's own idea for what disappointment is like. There could be a difference between the objectives that one has and the expectations involved. Understanding what disappointment is really like in one's mind can be essential for handling one's ideas and values. There is a need to think carefully about the definitions that will be used to ensure there are no problems with what one will be doing when resolving emotional problems.

Never Blame Others

The goal of cognitive psychology is to help people recognize what they are doing for themselves and how they can be better people without being hard on others. Much of this involves ensuring that other people are not blamed for the things that one might say or do. It is very easy to pass off the responsibility of a situation to someone else. Blaming is a frequent practice that is easy to do, but it only shows a lack of responsibility. It suggests that instead of being willing to accept a situation for what it is, someone will instead think more about the problems that have developed. The best thing to do in this situation is to be accepting of whatever has come one's way. It is not productive to blame others for everything that happens.

Never Be Overly Judgmental

It is understandable why people might be hard on themselves; they have their own worries or fears and they want to make what they are doing work well. The greatest problem is that being too harsh on oneself might make situations worse. Feelings of depression or anxiety often cause people to feel critical. People with these problems often feel as though they are defective and that they cannot be fixed properly. They might feel inferior to others due to the emotional struggles that they might have. The work that someone puts into CBT can only go so far as one wants it to go. Having a smart and useful plan on hand for therapy can make a real change in one's life.

Chapter 46 – Should a Psychiatrist Be Consulted?

Everything listed in this guide on cognitive behavioral therapy is simple and easy to follow on one's own. This could help people to manage their lives and emotions without having to consult a psychiatrist for help. That does not mean that a psychiatrist is always unnecessary. People who need emotional help might still require a psychiatrist for extra guidance in the cognitive psychology process. Many people are afraid to ask for this help because they are so concerned about their image. There are times when a psychiatrist needs to be consulted.

The Effort Is Overwhelming

The greatest problem is that the effort might be too intense and pervasive. That is, a person keeps on having to use the same strategies for managing one's mind all day long without stopping. This is a frustrating feeling, but it is a problem that will remain troubling and hard for many to live with. When that effort does not work does not produce results, it might be time to get in touch with a psychiatrist for added help.

Obsessions Become Too Prominent

CBT is to be used to help get people over their obsessive thoughts and allow new positive thoughts to come into play in one's life. There are often times when the obsessions could become too intense. The old worries that someone had might be so strong and a person will start to think too often about certain problems or worries in life. The obsessions might include obsessions to be perfect or to use the same thoughts even after an exercise is complete. Such a problem might be a sign of something a little more intense in one's mind and would, therefore, require a professional to provide more help in dealing with the obsession so that it does not take over a person's life.

Repeated Thoughts of Consulting a Therapist

Sometimes a person might continue to have thoughts of consulting a therapist even while using many of the strategies in this book. These thoughts might be a sign that someone is fearful of a process not working. It might suggest that a process is not as strong as one might have wished it could be. Persistent thoughts of consulting a therapist for help might be an indication that a therapist should be consulted.

People Talk About One's Need For a Psychiatrist

Even when someone tries to do things and change one's thinking, they might still have many visible problems that others may notice. The greatest problem here is that the person who needs help might not be fully aware of the problems that they have. Other people might notice the concerns that a person has, but the subject in question does not.

Anyone who hears requests about getting help should probably ask for that help.

Feelings Aren't Getting Better

Contacting a therapist is often a necessity for cases where the negative feelings one has are not changing. The points listed here should help people to change their lives and to make them feel stronger and more confident. When the traditional processes one uses are not working, it is best to consult a therapist for help. This is especially for cases where feelings of depression or other serious emotional problems continue to get worse and harder to manage.

Concerns about Medication

A person is not likely to require medications when talking with a psychiatrist. Many of today's psychiatrists are willing to help people find strategies for living that work without the need for any medications. Medication might still be prescribed for cases where a physical imbalance might appear in one's brain or a person's mental concerns are significant enough to where someone might be at a risk of self-harm. All psychiatrists focus on ensuring their patients are safe.

Conclusion

People who work to improve their lives are always trying to change their thoughts. By doing this, it becomes easier for the mind to grow and evolve. It is through one's emotional problems that one learns what can be done to get the problems one has managed. Cognitive psychology is a practice that helps people to understand how to thrive in life and make the work one puts in worthwhile. With CBT, a person will have more control over one's thoughts. The thoughts will be easy to manage because someone knows how to manage the positive ones and to keep the negative issues in one's mind from being a dramatic threat.

The fears that one might experience can be alleviated through CBT. The practice allows anyone to think twice about the fears one has and how they can hinder one's way of living a comfortable life. This includes an emphasis on knowing how fears are formed and how to gradually correct them before they can become a burden. CBT also works to relieve anxiety and for a person to recognize how irrational some anxiety-related triggers are. Many fears are not as strong as one might think and the anxieties produced by them are not things to be concerned about.

Some of the saddest feelings can be managed through CBT. Depression does not have to be a burden when the right ideas for regulating the mind and one's thoughts are introduced. Also, grief can be kept in check by using some smart ideas and constructive points to move on with life and to keep grief from crippling one's way of living. All of the points in this guide are suitable for many needs; they all require introspection and effort on a person's part to work. Those who are committed to the therapeutic process will find that it is not hard to get more out of the practice.

Be aware of how much time and control it might take to resolve certain emotional issues. Look at the work being put into the process and see what can be done to manage life in a constructive fashion. Always be aware of the situation one enters into and how challenging the problem might be as well. Every instance of how CBT may work varies by person, so knowing what to expect out of the process will be essential to one's success in keeping one's life in check.

Most importantly, be patient when using CBT. Every person responds to CBT uniquely. It might take weeks or even months to make cognitive progress. The effects of the process can last a lifetime and will allow a person to feel better about any situation one encounters. Good luck with using the points highlighted in this guide. It is easy to keep fears, depression, and other negative aspects of one's life from being overly influential when the best strategies and ideas for the concern are used.

A Preview of

Emotional Intelligence:

The Complete Guide to Improving Thoughts, Behavior, Relationships and Social Skills

(The EQ Book)

By Michael Garron

Chapter 1 – What Is Emotional Intelligence?

The emotions that people carry with them throughout the day are diverse. People can go from feeling happy to sad to excited to worried. Sometimes a person could experience all of these feelings in just a few hours.

These emotions are vital to everyone's life. The emotions that people have will dictate many of the things that they do. The things that people think and feel are always more powerful than the actions they do. It is vital for a person's emotional intelligence to be managed well. However, it is important for people who want to improve their EQ to understand what it entails and how it can be used.

The first thing to do when working with emotional intelligence is to understand what it is. Emotional intelligence is a vital part of life that all people need to possess if they are to be successful and strong-willed individuals.

Emotional intelligence refers to a person's ability to manage one's emotions and to handle the emotions of other people as well. It is about knowing what someone is feeling and having the ability to identify what makes those feel different. A universal sense of control is needed for making this part of one's life easy without adding anything frustrating to the relationship.

This concept is also known as the EQ or emotional quotient. It is different from the traditional intelligence quotient that is utilized to measure a person's intelligence.

Emotional intelligence has been a topic of interest to many businesses and organizations over the years. Although the concept of EQ was first introduced in the 1960s, it was not until the later part of the twentieth century that people began to take note of EQ. This happened because mental health and a person's ability to perform on the job have become very important considerations.

The Five Main Categories

There are five categories of emotional intelligence. The five points were introduced by Daniel Goleman, a prominent behavioral sciences expert. Goleman released these five-steps based on understanding what people can do to be stronger leaders in the workplace and to be more proficient in what they can do when helping others. The concepts continue to be important to this day:

1. Self-Awareness

This refers to how well a person is aware of emotions in one's self and other people. This includes having a clear idea of what people might feel when handling emotions and seeing what causes them to develop.

2. Self-Regulation

Self-regulation is the act of having control over one's emotions. This includes knowing how long an emotion will last and what can be done to keep an emotion from persisting.

3. Motivation

Motivation is how to use goals and efforts in one's life. This includes seeing what a person can do while using the right emotions to get where one wants to go.

4. Empathy

While emotional intelligence often focuses on knowing one's own emotions, empathy is knowing how others feel. This includes understanding what people are thinking and knowing how to react.

5. Social Skills

The ability to interact with people in a positive fashion is vital to one's success. A person with a high EQ will have the social skills needed to get along with others. This includes understanding how to manage nonverbal communications.

These five points will be discussed in their individual chapters throughout this guide.

EQ May Be More Important Than IQ

A good intelligence quotient or IQ is helpful for life. Knowing and understanding how to make logical and rational decisions is advantageous to everyone. At the same time, that IQ can only take people so far.

For instance, Jeffrey, a business executive has a very high IQ. He has thought of with many useful ideas for his business, and yet he is unable to get his business to expand or grow. He is having a hard time maintaining his payroll because people are constantly leaving the business.

Why is Jeffrey unable to get his business to grow? He is struggling with his EQ. He is not fully appreciative of his employees. Perhaps he does not understand that they need some balance between their work and their personal lives. This includes issues where workers are not satisfied with their jobs or are feeling too tired or uncomfortable with their work. But Jeffrey does not have the empathy to understand this.

As a result, it becomes hard for even his smartest ideas to thrive and grow. If he had a better EQ, he would make more plans based on what other people need. By adapting his ideas and values around what others want, it would become easier for his business to grow and thrive.

It is through one's EQ that it becomes easier to evolve and change.

What Makes It Different from Personality?

What makes EQ different from a person's standard personality? EQ focuses more on feelings while the personality is all about a person's style.

There are three things that make up every person:

1. The intelligence quotient
2. The emotional intelligence
3. General personality

Personality is hard-wired into one's brain. It is how a person would interact with others and behave in some fashion. Someone's personality can never change.

The EQ is different as a person can develop it over time. When a person is trained well, it becomes easier for that person to be active and positive. Many points about improving one's EQ will be covered throughout this guide to provide simple ideas for what they can do to get their lives to move forward.

A person's IQ is likely to stay the same throughout one's life. A person has a certain ability to learn things at a specific rate. It might be easier for a person to learn emotions and how to manage them if that person's IQ is not low.

EQ might be related to IQ when all is considered. When a person's EQ is high, it becomes easier for someone to want to learn. That person will use one's IQ to one's advantage. The emotions become balanced so that people fully understand what they can do to grow their lives. As a result, a person will use one's intelligence at a slightly better rate.

The emotional intelligence that a person holds is important for all people who want to accomplish the most in their workplaces.

Chapter 2 – What Makes EQ Special?

Emotional intelligence is more than just something relating to knowing what people feel. It is to understand and recognize what can be done to help others or to at least get along with them.

It is through a person's EQ that someone can get the most out of life. Anyone who has a high level of emotional intelligence will be more likely to succeed and thrive in one's work. There are several positives of one's EQ that must be explored. These points are vital for the workplace in particular as they relate to what people can do to move forward and thrive in their jobs.

Get Along With People

A workplace is often a challenging place. Each person brings their personalities, their biases, and their different levels of intelligence and experience to the work environment. They have to work in harmony and this is not always easy. There is also the added pressure of competition involved. Personal relationships outside of the workplace can be difficult at times as well. People often struggle with maintaining friendships. Finding a long-lasting romantic relationship can be challenging to some people.

Those with a high EQ are better equipped to get along with others. A high EQ individual will understand the ups and downs of relationships and make smart plans to avoid conflicts and to settle disagreements effectively.

Become More Productive

People who have a high EQ are more likely to be productive. Those people understand what they want out of their lives and aren't afraid of putting in the effort.

Let's say that there were two software engineers, Janet and Tom. They are working on the same task. Tom does not have much EQ and is not fully aware of what he wants to get out of his work. Janet is on the opposite end in that her EQ is high. Janet feels motivated in her work because she has her emotions in check. She knows how to identify what her co-workers are feeling and is capable of keeping negative emotions from persisting. She can produce her work easily. Tom is different as he is often worried about what will happen and is trapped in a mindset of uncertainty.

Janet will do more with her software engineering task because she is comfortable with herself. Her high EQ ensures she will find solutions for concerns she has about the work she is doing. All the added productivity allows someone to have more control over various functions and actions surrounding what one is doing in life. This, in turn, helps that person to feel emotionally positive about life. It becomes easier for many tasks to be done as one's emotions are kept in control.

People who are not emotionally intelligent will have a difficult time managing their thoughts, and this will keep them from being productive. A person might become overly worried when a new task is introduced and it is different from what one might be used to. A person with a low EQ might be afraid of what will happen if a project does not go right. All that worry and fear will cause a person to not do well with a task, thus falling into the trap of not knowing what to do to fix a problem or make things work right.

Stay Accountable

People often shift their responsibilities and try to keep things from being too complicated. They don't want to do things because they resist doing it, or maybe they are not aware of what to do to fix the problems that happen. Others might not be aware of the circumstances surrounding what they are doing.

Accountability is a necessity for people in any workplace. A person who is accountable for one's actions and work is not afraid to accept responsibility for their actions. It is through accountability that a person is capable of showing maturity and is able to recognize the duties and functions one has to enter into every day. This includes not only what is done correctly but also any errors that might occur. A person with a strong EQ will be more likely to stay accountable.

Accountability provides a person with the ability to take control of a situation. That person will understand that he or she is doing something valuable or necessary. By working with the right plans, it becomes easy for a person to stay accountable and confident with what one is going to do with life.

Easier to Manage Risks

There are risks to everything in life. A person might get into a car and go driving to the grocery store, but that someone is getting into the risk that the car will malfunction or someone might cause an accident on the road. Meanwhile, a person who plays gridiron football might enjoy playing it, but that individual has the risk of suffering a substantial injury like a concussion.

There are risks involved in every aspect of every workplace. One of the greatest reasons why errors are often made in the workplace is because workers are not fully aware of the risks and what they can do to lessen them. This can cause people to panic when something happens they did not anticipate. They might not have the emotional fortitude to handle some of the events that occur. Those who can handle and figure out their emotions will have an easier time moving forward and keeping everything under control.

A person's emotional intelligence can be utilized to figure out what one's abilities are and how well certain tasks may be completed. Knowing what can be done to fix issues and having a plan for emergencies is essential.

Avoid Questions

When a person has a low emotional intelligence, they are not certain about the decisions they made. They lack self-confidence. One of the most common questions that a person might ask is what he or she was thinking about in the past? For instance, a man who made a difficult move in the past might ask himself, "What was I thinking? I can't believe I did something that way. Why did I do that?" That man would have failed to use his emotional intelligence. People make rash decisions when they are not thinking about the results or consequences. They might think about the results that they want to attain, but they never think about why they want it or what they can do to maintain those results.

Emotional intelligence is needed to help people to have faith in what they are deciding to do. People need emotional intelligence to stay comfortable and focused on whatever it is they want to work on. More importantly, there will be less confusion when a person's EQ is strong. That person will not question their own decisions. People with a high EQ will not likely ask questions of other people in the workplace or in other situations. A person who asks lots of questions is revealing their low self-esteem and low self-confidence.

A Matter of Trust

People are loyal to people that they trust. One person might seem to be more intelligent than another, but what if that smarter person is difficult for people to trust? That intelligent person might be seen as stubborn or difficult to work with. An intelligent person might not have the emotional intelligence needed to deal with people. When EQ is missing, that person is not capable of understanding or having empathy toward others. But when a person has a high emotional intelligence, that person becomes easier to trust. This leads to added success and control over any situation.

It is through a trust that people can stay positive around others. When people trust each other, they are willing to support one another through anything that might come about in the workplace. Trust focuses on people showing that they recognize each other's emotions and are willing to support each other. People who trust one another are likely to get along and feel better in each other's company.

Without trust, it becomes hard for a business to grow and thrive. More importantly, a personal or romantic relationship will not get off the ground if the people involved do not trust each other.

Managing Customers

An interesting part of working with EQ is that it concentrates on how well people are able to interact with each other in a workplace. This includes working with customers in a smart manner.

It is easier for businesses to grow when its employees have EQ. An employee needs a high EQ to have a sense of empathy with customers. When a person understands the emotions of others it becomes easier for that someone to market a product. Having an understanding of emotions is vital for success. This is especially true of the workplace when customers are involved. Every customer should be treated with respect and care to ensure there are no problems that can't be dealt with.

Let's say that Sally is working to sell a car. She might notice that a customer is nervous about the process of buying a car. She can empathize with the customer and talk with that person about the process. Sally might explain what makes a car an attractive investment. She may also identify questions that people have and provide smart answers to those issues. By using her EQ, Sally is getting in touch with the customer and is showing that she cares about that customer's needs. This will make it easier for her to sell the car to that customer.

It is through the EQs of its employees that relationships with customers can be built. When the employees are capable of working with customers well, it becomes easier for people to feel comfortable with each other while doing business.

A Vital Foundation for Other Skills

The emotional intelligence that one has is the foundation of many skills. A person who has a high EQ will have many great skills:

- Time management – A person will know how to handle one's time and budget certain times of the day for specific tasks.

- Decision-making – People with high EQ can make the smartest possible decisions.

- Communication – It is a necessity for a person to communicate with others. A high EQ is often associated with strong communication skills.

- Stress tolerance – Those who do not have a high EQ will break down under stress. A person might not have an ability to manage certain ideas or actions because that person is incapable of handling the associated stress.

- Anger management – People who do not have control over their emotions are more likely to become angry because they don't know what to do. When someone has a high EQ, those emotions are easier to manage and allow a person control over situations.

- Presentation – It will be easier to use one's presentation skills to one's advantage if the person has a high EQ. The presentation is closely associated with the ability to communicate effectively.

By having a high EQ, a person has an ability to handle many things in one's life without struggling.

www.ingramcontent.com/pod-product-compliance
Lightning Source LLC
Chambersburg PA
CBHW051528020426
42333CB00016B/1835